Chosen as One of Ohio's
BEST
of the
BEST
COOKBOOKS
by Quail Ridge Press

Voted by North American
Bookdealers Exchange as
**"1996 Best Book
of the
YEAR"**
in the Category of
Cooking

"We truly can enjoy good food that is also low in fat. The recipes in *Down Home Cookin'* are perfect examples of just such recipes."

> JoAnna Lund
> Food Writer and Author
> Healthy Exchanges, Inc.

"This cookbook has been a wonderful tool for people trying to adjust to their new lifestyle after their cardiac event."

> Samantha Christie, R.N.
> Cardiac Rehab Nurse

"As a leader for First Peace (a diet class), Dawn Hall's cookbook has been a valuable tool in helping my ladies lose weight and very successfully also! Our potluck rule is just bring anything out of *Down Home Cookin' Without the Down Home Fat!*"

> Kathy Rahla
> Leader, First Peace
> (Weight Loss Class)

"The *Down Home Cookin'* cookbook has been a Godsend. My family has truly enjoyed the unique recipes. They are easy to prepare and healthy for you. They have helped reduce the fat in our diets which in turn is helping us to lose weight."

> Cheryl A. Oedy
> Homemaker

Down Home Cookin' Without the Down Home Fat

by

Dawn Hall

Trade Life Books
Tulsa, Oklahoma

A portion of the author's profits from this book will go to Toledo's Solid Rock Outreach Program, focusing on the needs of inner-city children. On behalf of the children, the author thanks you for your support.

Down Home Cookin' Without the Down Home Fat
ISBN 1-57757-018-9
Copyright © 1996 by Dawn Hall
5425 South Fulton-Lucas Road
Swanton, Ohio 43558

Published by Trade Life Books
P. O. Box 55325
Tulsa, Oklahoma 74155

Contents

Dedication

Though I give God all of the praise and glory for the success of this book, it is my courageous and wonderful husband, Tracy Hall, to whom it is dedicated. The long hours of hard work it took to create this cookbook seem so insignificant in comparison to the grueling challenges he has so bravely endured. As he courageously fights cancer each day, he continues to exemplify a true godly man by being a terrific human being, husband, and father. He never ceases to amaze me with his perseverance, determination, and commitment to God and life itself. One of the greatest blessings of my life is having Tracy as my husband.

I told Tracy the day after his thirty-second birthday (when we found out he had brain cancer) that I believed God would use our challenging circumstances for good. To this day, God has!

A Special Note of Thanks

I wholeheartedly believe this book is a gift from God, so of course I want to thank Him.

Second, I want to thank my wonderful husband, Tracy, who never complained about all the flops I created. I know I owe him more than a thousand dollars for all of the food I've ruined.

A big thank you to all of my students in my water aerobics and W.O.W. (Watching Our Weight) classes who constantly encouraged me to start writing this cookbook.

To all of my friends, family, and students, thank you for being my taste-tester guinea pigs! I appreciate your truthfulness in letting me know which ones you liked and did not like.

I would like to thank two wonderful cookbook authors. These truly professional women reached out and offered a hand to a "new girl on the block" in the industry. It is with the utmost respect and admiration that I thank JoAnna Lund of "Heavenly Exchanges" for her wisdom, guidance, and direction, and Pam Mycoskie for her knowledge, insight, and sincere, caring love toward me and my family.

A special thank you to Cynthia Beekley, one of my editors — and my favorite English teacher!

Thanks again, everybody!

Introduction

I feel like I was born on a diet! I can't remember a time when I didn't have to watch my weight. At times it felt like all I had to do was look at a magazine ad with fattening, delicious-looking food on it and I'd gain five pounds. Needless to say, watching my weight has been very, very frustrating. I wish I could tell you, now that I've written this book, that my weight is no longer a challenge for me, but it still is. However, maintaining a comfortable weight is much easier now that I've learned to cook in a healthier way. I will never be *skinny*, but healthy and fit, yes!

Things really turned around for me when I realized that the dictionary does not define the word *diet* as starvation or depravation! Diet is what we eat and drink — food and liquid. Everyone consumes a diet. The key is to learn what constitutes a healthy diet.

From that point on, I have never been on a "diet." Yes, I watch what I eat, and when I want to lose a few extra fat pounds, I increase my walking or aerobic time, while cutting back on the amount of calories I consume. But I keep eating the same foods all the time. I know that the foods I eat to lose excess fat are the same foods I continue eating to maintain my weight. Although I'll never be a "skinny-minny," I know I no longer have to fear being a "fatty-patty!"

Moderation Is the Key

The Bible instructs us to train our children "in the way they should go." (See Proverbs 22:6.) I believe that includes everything in life: spiritual, mental, emotional — and physical. The saying, "We are what we eat," is valid because what we eat affects our energy level and our emotional well-being, as well as our health and weight. However, eating "no fat" doesn't guarantee you will not be fat.

There are loads and loads of fat-free and low-fat products flooding around the market today. Many of them are as fattening as can be, loaded down with sugars and sweeteners. You can eat more low-fat foods to reach 3,000 calories than high-fat foods (gram vs. gram), but the truth is, you're still eating 3,000 calories, and you can get fat! Calories are calories.

The ultimate difficult truth is that we need to lower the number of calories our bodies maintain daily. We can do that by increasing our exercise time, decreasing our intake of calories, or both. Yes, it is easier to lower your calories by eating fat-free and low-fat foods, but if you're eating too many calories, you're eating too many calories and you won't lose fat. Too much of any good thing — even fat-free, low-fat food — is too much!

Don't get me wrong, I don't encourage eating high-fat foods! But I do want to set the record straight. Eating too much, no matter how healthy the food, is eating too much, period. It's a difficult fact, but a true one. Moderation is the key and that's something I still struggle with daily.

Remembering that moderation is the key enables me to enjoy foods I used to *never* eat without feeling guilty and ashamed. You know what I'm talking about! Occasionally, I give myself freedom to wander — in moderation — with a piece of chocolate or a few potato chips. And I stress the fact that I consciously choose to wander from a low-fat, high-fiber, healthy diet *in moderation*.

You may "choose to wander" on special occasions and holidays for example. But choosing to wander doesn't mean going "hog-wild," eating all the junk food and sweets we would like until our stomachs are so full that they ache. It means choosing to have a little of something that you would normally not eat.

Along with moderation, it's important to learn which foods are "trouble" foods for you. Trouble foods are those that "get me goin'" — foods that are hard to stop eating once I taste them. A trouble food for you may not be a trouble food for someone else, but don't buy them, even if they are for someone else in the family. Why? Even if you're feeling strong when you buy them and have no intention of eating them, when your guard is down and you're feeling weak, your body will be screaming to indulge in "just a little piece." Before you know it, you will have consumed numerous little pieces. And then what happens? Guilt city! It's just not worth it!

Locate your weaknesses and guard against situations and people that might cause you to give in to them. This will help you to grow into a stronger and better human being.

Well! What About Fat?

I love to create in the kitchen! The first year we were married, my husband and I never ate the same thing for dinner twice. I took pride in never allowing my husband's meals to be boring. On our first wedding anniversary, we asked each other what we could do to become a better spouse. My husband Tracy said, "Honey, could you just cook the same meal twice, at least once this year?"

I laughed! My meat and potatoes man wanted plain ol' meals! But making tasty, exciting meals — whether they were just meat and potatoes or something exotically gourmet — also seemed to mean a lot of fat.

Fat! Fat! Fat! Aren't you sick of it? It can be frustrating to live with it, and you can't live without it! I'm not a doctor, nor do I pretend to know all they know, but I do have a lot of personal experience with the yucky stuff. As a recovering compulsive eater, an aerobic instructor, and a facilitator of self-help groups such as W.O.W. (Watching Our Weight), I do know quite a bit about fat. As a teacher, it seems only natural for me to share with you briefly, in layman's terms, what I know about fat. So I'm going to K.I.S.S. the subject lightly. (K.I.S.S. = Keep It Simple, Sweetie!)

Our bodies need fat (approximately 10 grams per day) for healthy skin, hair, nails, etc. Ten grams is such a tiny bit that most of us can consume the fats we need naturally without *ever* adding a bit of fat to the preparation of our food — *ever*! I don't even have oil, real butter, margarine, or other such products in our home. We just don't need them!

There are good fats and bad fats, but the truth is, fats are fattening no matter what type of fat they are. Although olive oil is less harmful than margarine, butter, and other alternatives, it's still not good for you if you are trying to reduce your fat intake. Dietary fat is the most concentrated form of calories. Fats have 9 calories per gram, protein or carbohydrates have 4 calories per gram, and alcohol has 7 calories per gram. (A gram is a weight measurement.)

Refraining from fats, ounce for ounce, you can consume a larger quantity of food for your calories. Dietary fat is more easily turned into body fat once eaten because, of all the calories, it is most like our bodies' fat. Now you know what the saying, "Over the lips onto the hips," truly means! For the heart-conscious, health-conscious, and weight-conscious person, avoiding dietary fat is helpful (but not the cure-all) for maintaining a healthy, desirable weight.

Most people know that lowering their fat intake is helpful in reducing heart disease.[1] The incidence of heart disease has been drastically reduced since the public became aware of this fact. Once again the statement, "We are what we eat," has a lot of validity. Choosing to "wander" occasionally is okay, as long as it doesn't become the "norm." Science has proven that a 10 percent fat diet can even reverse heart disease.[2]

What a lot of people are not aware of is that cancer thrives on fats too! Cancer is the generic name given to more than 100 different diseases, which have a common factor: they like fats and refined sugars. Reducing your consumption of fats not only lowers your risk of heart disease but also cancer.[3]

What about fat? If more than 30 percent of your daily calorie intake is from fat calories, it is not a good thing!

---

[1] *Controlling Your Fat Intake*, by Joseph C. Piscatella (New York: Workman Publishing, 1991) p. 5.

[2] *Dr. Dean Ornish's Program for Reversing Heart Disease*, by Dr. Dean Ornish (New York: Ballantine Books, 1992) and *Pritikin Program Diet and Exercise*, by Nathan Pritikin and Patrick McGrady (New York: Grosset & Dunlap, 1979).

[3] *Beating Cancer With Nutrition*, by Dr. Patrick Quillin (Tulsa: The Nutrition Press, 1994), pp. 18, 39, 46.

I'm Sick of the Lies!!!

Manufacturers know that people are more health conscious these days and want to eat healthier. So what do the manufacturers do? A lot of them lie! Don't take the manufacturer's word that the product is "low-fat." READ the nutrition label! This is an *absolute must*! For those of you who are hard of learning, repeat after me:

"I, (put your name here) will not buy any product without first looking at the nutrition label on the package! As a responsible person I am going to know up front exactly how many fats and calories I will be consuming. I am not going to fall for their lies!!!"

_____

(*Signature*)

In layman's terms, I'm going to tell you how to read a nutrition label on food containers. But first, let's confirm up front that I'm talking primarily about fats. I'm not talking about sodium, although I do not encourage adding table salt to food. (There is already more than enough salt in the food we eat). I am also not addressing fiber, although we should try to get at least 25-30 grams per day. My primary focus here is fats.

Believe me when I tell you, "Things are not always as they seem."

A perfect example is Kraft Macaroni and Cheese (the kind you add milk to). Sounds terrible, right? Wrong! As far as fat is concerned, it's okay. A 5.5-ounce box has two servings — a nice-sized portion, 260 calories per serving, and only 3 grams of fat. What makes it fattening is that milk and margarine are added. If fat-free margarine or liquid Butter Buds and skim milk are used, the fat calories remain low.

On the other hand, so-called "healthy" products, such as convenient microwave meals that claim to be low-fat, can be high in fat, containing up to 9 grams of fat for one small meal! Check it out!

Another thing that cracks me up is the calculation of the portion size. Even some authors of so-called low-fat cookbooks get their fats and calories low per serving because they reduce the normal portion size down to some inky-dinky piece! PLEASE!!! We're not birds!

If you're eating a so-called low-fat dessert prepared in a 9 x 13-inch pan, and the recipe says it has 36 servings, you can bet your bottom dollar that's an itty-bitty serving size! (I would call it a taste, not a serving!) Yes, it may be slightly under 100 calories, but multiply that by the number of servings you'll probably eat to feel satisfied (2-3) and you've just eaten 200-300 calories! Again, don't be fooled! Check out your portion size.

Lifestyle Principles for Overall Health

The following are things which, when practiced consistently over time, will help you feel good and stay fit:

- Wake up at least five minutes earlier than you need to. Thank God for all He's done for you and spend time with Him. Thanking Him will lift your spirits and help you start your day with the right attitude.

- Before getting out of bed, take a few moments and *visualize* yourself succeeding in taking overall good care of yourself. Visualize yourself eating low-fat snacks and meals, and feeling satisfied. Also visualize yourself exercising regularly. Remember: what you think about, you bring about!

- Take time for at least one-half hour of aerobic *exercise* at least three times a week, if not more. This is a perfect time for building relationships and improving your emotional health. I think fewer people would need to see counselors and therapists if they shared their feelings with good friends. I find that walking and talking with a good friend is a wonderful experience. It's like getting a two-for-one deal! I like to cross train (do a different exercise daily). I walk, bike, dance, or do step aerobics. It adds spice to my life. Studies show that people who enjoy the type of exercise they're doing are more apt to stick with it. The key is to find what you enjoy and do it.

- Manage your time wisely. Don't overbook, and give yourself plenty of time to accomplish each task. If you think it's going to take ten minutes to get there, give yourself fifteen so you aren't under so much pressure. I have to work on this one daily. As an overachiever, I tend to overbook — which is extremely stressful!

- Think only positive thoughts. If an idea is not positive, *get rid of it!* Negative thoughts can bring you down before you even realize it — so don't give room to them. And don't hang around with negative people who do! Life is too short and has too much to offer to be wasting time being negative.

- If at all possible, don't go to bed angry, anxious, or upset — especially with family and close friends. Peaceful sleep is tremendously important for the maintenance and repair of a healthy body. If you need to apologize to your child, clear the air with a friend, or get something straight with your spouse, make time for it before bedtime. Then sleep in peace!

Tricks of the Trade

The following are my "tricks of the trade" for eating nutritionally:

- The first thing you've got to do is "DE-FAT" your house! I know this is tough because I did it when I first started eating extremely low fat. But listen to me. "You've gotta do it!" There are no ifs, ands, or buts about it! Fat is not good for you, it's not good for your children, and I don't care if your spouse is as skinny as a rail, he doesn't need it either! Fat is fat. Period! Get it out. Mayo, oils, junk food, fatty red meats! Pitch it! Believe me, as a penny counter all my life, I know it's hard to throw away that money. All I can say is, "Just Do It!" It's going to cost you a lot more in the long run (mentally, emotionally, and physically) if you don't.

- Go to your favorite grocery store and stock up on fat-free products. There are many to choose from, and I've enclosed my favorites in this book. This is an easy rule of thumb — if there are more than 3 grams of fat per 100 calories, don't eat it. To be honest, I think that's even too much, but the American Heart Association endorses a 30 percent or less intake of dietary fat. Personally, I try to stick to 20 grams of fat a day, which is approximately 10 percent of my calories per day. For optimum health, that is the standard I set for myself.

- If you can't "go cold turkey," then make your changes gradually. Milk is a biggy. A lot of people who've grown up on whole milk have a hard time making the switch to skim. Here is what I encourage my classes to do if they're having a hard time making the switch.

  1st week — $^1/_2$ whole milk and $^1/_2$ - 2% milk mixed

  2nd week — 2% milk

  3rd week — $^1/_2$ — 2% milk and $^1/_2$ - 1% milk

  4th week — 1% milk

  5th week — $^1/_2$ - 1% milk and $^1/_2$ skim milk

  6th week — skim milk!

  There, that wasn't so bad after all — was it?

Surprising facts:

Whole milk — Approximately $1/2$ fat!

2% milk — Approximately $1/3$ fat

Skim milk — 0 fat!!!! WOW!!!

- When cooking, chew mint gum. It helps keep me from tasting. (If that doesn't work, tape your mouth shut!)

- Hurry! Wash off those fingers! *Don't lick them clean!*

- If you're journaling daily what you eat, add 25 calories per small taste for low-fat foods and 50 calories per taste for high-fat foods! You'll be surprised how fast those calories add up!

- Plan on spending one hour each week cleaning fresh veggies and fruits after grocery shopping. I can guarantee having veggies and fruit prepared for easy eating will increase consumption dramatically! Let's face it, when you want a quick snack the last thing you feel like doing is peeling a carrot! A clever idea is cut veggies into bite-sized pieces for salads and put them in a relish tray. I refrigerate prepared veggies so that when I'm preparing a salad, all I have to do is sprinkle whatever veggies I want onto the salad.

- Take a large plastic cake container and turn it upside down. Using three large heads of dark green lettuce (leafy, romaine, etc.), prepare a large salad of *greens* only. Only garnish with bite-sized veggies prepared in relish tray (mentioned earlier) once ready to serve salad.

- For relishes, I cut the veggies into "finger food" size and put them into another relish tray. For quick dips, I use favorite fat-free salad dressings.

- Fruits — fresh melons, pineapples, and berries can be cleaned and stored for up to five or six days. I like to put these in relish trays or Ziploc bags. Allow fresh fruit to sit out on the counter. Hopefully a healthy, fresh visual will be more enticing than an ol' prepackaged processed snack. (If not, at least it was a good try!)

- Studies show that people who are most successful at maintaining a healthier lifestyle are those who have a strong support system. If your friends and family won't be there for you, then consider belonging to a self-help group where you'll find people who will.

- If someone absolutely insists on having something that is totally fattening and practically irresistible to you in the house, then by all means be honest with them and assertively ask them to hide it and not eat it in front of you. My husband used to love a certain brand of barbecue chips. The problem was, I did too! I would eat 12 chips and gain 10 pounds (okay — maybe I really didn't, but it felt like it! And anyway, who can eat only 12?) I asked him to keep them in his truck. That way he had them for his lunch and I wasn't being tortured by some measly little 5-ounce bag in my pantry screaming, "Eat me! Eat me!"

- I encourage people who are trying to live a healthier lifestyle to express their needs in what I call a "win-win" way. That is, be assertive in expressing your needs, while respecting the other person's needs. Assertive communication means being open and honest in a thoughtful and tactful way. The "Golden Rule" (treat others the way you want to be treated) is a great rule of thumb. When you do this, you can work out a compromise like Tracy and I did over barbecue chips.

- Another trick that gets me through challenging times (when I'm away from home) is keeping fat-free snacks in the trunk of my car. Because I do this, I don't have to worry about being at a carry-out or gas station's mercy. By keeping a variety of fat-free snacks I like in the trunk, I always know I'm prepared if I become hungry.

- To avoid overeating, do not eat while driving or watching TV. I do *NOT* "eat and drive." If I do eat something from the trunk of my car, I take a few moments, turn the engine off, and sit in the car. I make myself "enjoy the moment." Let's face it. Eating is orally stimulating, and while eating your body releases chemicals that produce a calming effect. (It's easy to see why people become food addicts.) When we "eat on the run," we deprive ourselves of the complete eating experience, it is less fulfilling, and we are apt to crave more afterwards.

- Serve only as much as you think you will eat. Serve appropriate portions by putting food on plates. Serving family style (with bowls on the table) encourages overeating. Haven't we all at one time or another eaten a second helping of something just because it was there staring us in the face?

- Make a double of what you'll need and freeze the remaining portion for a "quick meal" down the road, or pack it for tomorrow's lunches.

- When I worked full time, I liked cooking for the week on Saturdays. It saved me time and with microwaves was convenient.

- Always remember, moderation is the key. To say I'll never eat a barbecue chip in my life is to set myself up for failure, because I can choose to wander now and then. I just have to be careful not to let wandering become a habit.

Grocery Shopping

The supermarket can be a dreadful experience if you aren't prepared. Besides watching labels and following a grocery list, consider these helpful hints:

- Carry a basket instead of pushing a cart if you don't need a lot of items. With your arms full of products, you are less likely to buy compulsively.

- If you are pushing a cart, leave it at the end of what would be considered a "danger zone." You know what I mean — the aisles that are loaded with high-fat, scrumptious, tantalizing products that are hard to resist. At times it seems like those hard-to-resist products are calling out, "Buy me! Buy me! You know you want me!" I hate those aisles! Wouldn't it be nice and a whole lot less stressful if all supermarket aisles were as easy to go down as the cleaning or paper products aisle? If you don't push your cart down that horrendous fat-loaded aisle, you will be a lot less likely to grab other products, since your hands will be full carrying what you need. Just put blinders on, go directly to the product you're looking for, and get out of there fast!

- If you see your favorite "weakness" high-fat item on sale, walk away as fast as you can! Let's pretend we see our favorite chocolate bar on sale. It's an unbelievable sale! One thousand candy bars for only a buck! WOW! It's only natural to start to rationalize giving in to this absolutely fabulous temptation.... "I'll only eat $1/4$ of the bar (about 3 grams of fat) for the next eleven years. Yeah! That's a good idea!" I call a situation like this a "red flag." Whenever you see a potential red flag, tell yourself, "No!" and get away from it as soon as possible. Hopefully the old saying, "Out of sight, out of mind," will be true. If you give in to that moment of weakness, however, you'll regret it! You're paying way too high a price ($1.00 for this situation) for a lot of grief, frustration, anxiety, and stress! Do yourself a favor — don't buy it!

- Watch prices! Manufacturers love to market products as fat-free and then double the price. Often you can find a similar product for a lot less. I refuse to pay double just because it has 1 gram of fat less than a less expensive product. Pretzel manufacturers love to do this. Compare and save.

Saving Money With Coupons

Let's face it, for the most part, fat-free products are more expensive than their counterparts. I feel it's worth peace of mind and better health to pay the extra cost. When I have time, I do "the coupon thing." For a $5.00 investment, my coupon book has saved me a lot of grief, time, and money. I get so many compliments on my coupon organization and it is *a lot* less stressful than sorting through them, so I'm sharing it with you. Here's what you'll need:

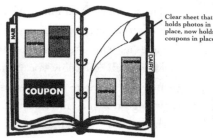

Clear sheet that holds photos in place, now holds coupons in place.

• 100-page large photo album with clear film sheets that hold photos in place

• 1 envelope with flap cut off

• tape

• coupons

• tabs (used for filing)

Label tabs individually for easy finding. I label mine: Dairy, Breads, Meats, Fish, Chicken, Cleaning Supplies, Hair Care, etc. Each section will have its own title page. Tape labeled tabs onto outside edge of photo album pages so that you can easily go to any section desired. (Only one tab per page. There will be numerous pages without tabs in each section following title page.)

Put coupons in proper sections.

Cut flap off the envelope. Tape the envelope to the front inside cover of the photo album. Put coupons you've pulled from the designated sections in an envelope for easy storage until check-out time. I also put rebates into the envelope.

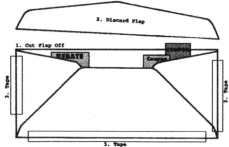

What I Like to Stock in My Kitchen

There are literally hundreds (if not thousands) of fat-free and very low-fat products on the market today. The problem (as I'm sure a lot of you know) is that many do *NOT* taste good! The other day I tried a new fat-free potato chip. Yuck! I'm telling you, the bag it was packaged in had to taste better than the product! It was terrible!

Have no fear! The following is a list of products I enjoy using. Look for them in your grocery store, and have confidence they will taste better than the packaging!

An easy rule of thumb when reading labels: if it has more than 3 grams of fat per 100 calories, don't buy it, don't use it, and pitch it! The only time I break that rule is for super lean beef such as:

Type of Beef	Serving Size	Fat Grams	Calories	% Fat Calories
London Broil/ Flank Steak	3 oz.	6	167	32%
Top Loin (Lean Only)	3 oz.	6	162	33%
Eye of Round (As a steak, roast or have butcher grind for super lean hamburger)	3 oz.	5	150	30%

If you enjoy eating red meat and do not want to refrain, then I encourage you to make the switch to ground eye of round. You'll be doing your heart, health, and waistline a *lot* of good!

The second time I break the rule is when I "choose to wander." An example might be a small piece of chocolate. Remember, this is done *very rarely*!

(Note: I am not a big fan of fat-free cheeses or margarines, but in my recipes, they taste good.)

Butter & Margarines

Butter Buds
 (found in spice or diet section)
Butter-flavored Pam Spray
Non-fat cooking sprays
 (generic brands are fine)
I Can't Believe It's Not Butter
 Spray
Ultra Fat-free Promise
 Margarine

Breads & Grains

Aunt Millie's breads & buns
Enriched flour
Father Sam's Kangaroo Bread
Flour tortillas fat-free
 (Buena Vista is good)
Graham crackers
Health Valley fat-free cookies
Health Valley fat-free granola
 (I use for my homemade
 granola bars)
Italian seasoned bread crumbs
Lite breads with 40 calories and
 no fat per slice (Aunt Millie's,
 Bunny, and Wonder are good)
Nabisco Reduced Fat Ritz
 Crackers
Oyster crackers
Pastas (except egg noodles;
 pastas from whole durum
 wheat are best)
Pillsbury Buttermilk Biscuits
Pillsbury Pizza Crust
Quaker Rice Cakes (caramel
 and strawberry flavored)
Quick cooking oats
Rice (whole grain enriched)
Rightshape Biscuits
 (buttermilk flavor)

Breads & Grains, cont'd.

Vegetable bread
Whole grain and white rice
Whole wheat flour

Beverages

Bottled water (don't be fooled
 by flavored waters; a lot of
 them are loaded with sugar and
 calories)
Cider
Country Time Lemonade
 (sugar free)
Crystal Light (sugar free)
Dole fruit juices (100%)
Grapefruit juice (100%)
Kool-Aid (sugar free)
Orange juice (100%)
Prune juice (100%)
Tea (instant or tea bag)
Tomato juice
Virgin Mary juice

Cheese

(To be honest with you, I do not
 like fat-free cheese, but used
 properly in recipes they can
 taste delicious!)
Blue cheese
Healthy Choice fat-free cheese
 (my favorite brand)
Italian topping (grated)
Parmesan (grated)
Ricotta (fat-free)

Condiments

Almond extract
Braum's fat-free fudge topping
Coconut extract
Cornstarch
Dressings (fat-free)
Equal
Evaporated skim milk (Lite)
Hidden Valley Reduced Calorie
  Dry Salad Dressing Mix
Honey
Karo Syrup
Kraft Free Mayonnaise and
  Miracle Whip
Kroger fat-free ice cream
  toppings
Liquid smoke
°Lite syrups
  (I like Mrs. Butterworth's)
Mint extract
Mrs. Richardson's fat-free
  ice cream toppings
Mustard
Not So Sloppy Joe Mix
NutraSweet
°Pam spray
  (non-fat cooking spray)
Preserves and jellies (low sugar)
Smucker's fat-free toppings
Lite soy sauce
Taco seasoning mix
Lite teriyaki marinade
Tomato sauce
Vanilla

° The generic brands of these
  items are less expensive and
  good.

Dairy

Buttermilk (non-fat)
Cottage cheese (non-fat)
  (I like all of them)
Dry powdered milk (non-fat)
  (best used in recipes — I don't
  care to drink it)
Evaporated skim milk
Flavorite fat-free yogurts and
  non-fat cottage cheese
Frozen yogurt (be careful, some
  are loaded with calories
  because of high sugar content!)
Skim milk
Fat-free sour cream (I like Land
  O Lakes or Light & Lively)
Fat-free yogurts (watch labels —
  high sugar content means high
  calorie count)
Healthy Indulgence (Kroger
  grocery stores' name brand)
  fat-free cheeses, yogurts, etc.

Fruits and Veggies

Applesauce
Canned vegetables —
  no salt added
Canned fruits in fruit juice only
All fresh vegetables (except for
  avocado — major fat!!)
All frozen vegetables and fruits
  with *no* sugar added
Cranberry sauce
Lite fruit cocktail
Lite pie fillings — cherry,
  blueberry, apple (The generic
  brand pie fillings taste fine)
Hot chili beans (I like
  Brook's brand)

Junk Food

(Usually no fat, but still too much sugar or salt to eat a lot of.) Caramel corn (most brands are only 1 fat gram but high in sugar content)

Entenmann's fat-free baked goods

Frito Lay Potato Crisps (new potato chip substitute) (They're delicious — if you like Pringles you'll like these! Only 1.5 fat grams per 100 calories — about 12 chips)

Frozen fat-free yogurts

Hostess "Lite" twinkies and brownies (It's hard to believe they're really low fat.)

Jello fat-free pudding and pudding cups

Keebler Elfin Delights

Little Debbie's Lite Oatmeal Pies and Brownies (new)

Marshmallows

Pepperidge Farm Fat-free Brownies and Blondies (too good!)

Pretzels

Betty Crocker Pop Chips

Rice cakes (Quaker strawberry and caramel flavored)

Smart Pop microwave popcorn (Orville Redenbacher)

SnackWell's cookies

Baked Tostitos, Salsa & Cream Cheese, Cool Ranch, and Regular flavors

Meats, Fish, Poultry

Beef (eye of round, London broil, flank steak, top loin)

Canadian bacon

Chicken breast (no skin; dark meat has twice as much fat!)

Crab meat flake or stick (imitation)

Eckrich fat-free meats (hot dogs, lunch meats, smoked sausage, Kielbasa)

Fish (the white ones are lower in fats; i.e., flounder, grouper, pike, sole, cod, orange roughy, monk fish, perch, scallops)

Hot dogs (Healthy Choice — 1 fat gram; Hormel Light & Lean — 1 fat gram; Oscar Mayer — fat-free)

Shellfish (Lobster, Crab, Shrimp)

Tuna (packed in water)

Turkey breast (no skin; dark meat has twice as much fat!)

Other Items

Dream Whip

Eggs (use only the whites)

Egg Beaters

Cool Whip Free

Pre-Packaged Items

Applesauce (sugar-free is lower in calories)

Betty Crocker "Lite" Cake, Brownie, Bread & Muffin Mixes

Boullion cubes (chicken, beef, and vegetable flavors)

Other Items, cont'd.

Campbell's Healthy Request
low-fat and fat-free soups and
sauces
Gold Medal Fudge Brownie Mix
Healthy Indulgence
(Kroger's name brand) fat-free
cheeses, yogurts, etc.
Health Valley Chili and Soups
Healthy Choice soups and sauces
(low- and no-fat)
Instant mashed potatoes
Jiffy cake mixes
Legumes (Beans — canned or
dry variety and lentils)
Martha White's Lite mixes
(muffins, etc.)
Old El Paso fat-free refried beans
Pancake and buttermilk
pancake Mix
Pasta
Pillsbury Lovin' Lites brownie,
cake, and muffin Mixes
Pillsbury Lovin' Lites frostings
Special K Fat-free Waffles
Chef Boy-R-Dee Spaghetti O's
Stuffing mixes (look for brands
that have only 2 fat grams per
serving as packaged)

Sauces

Healthy Choice Spaghetti Sauce
Heinz Homestyle Lite gravies
(in a jar)
Pepperidge Farm Stroganoff
Gravy
Prego spaghetti and pizza sauces
(Lite ones)
Ragu Pizza Quick Sauce
Ragu Today's Recipe spaghetti
sauces (low fat)

Miscellaneous Notes to the Cook
Kids' Cookin' Recipes

When you see this Kids' Cookin' logo, it means the recipe is *child appropriate*. Most children will be able to make it with a minimum of adult supervision.

Sugar Substitutes

I do not encourage the use of *Equal* and *NutraSweet*, which are registered trademarks of the NutraSweet Company, or *Sweet and Low*. None of these products have sponsored or are otherwise connected with this publication. However, I feel it is important to provide an alternative for those who are diabetic. For more information, you might call: NutraSweet Hotline 1-800-321-7254.

Brand Names

Most brand names used in this book are registered trademarks and are thus protected by law.

Butter Buds

This is a boxed butter flavor substitute found in the spice section of most grocery stores. To make liquid Butter Buds, simply follow the directions on the box and add water to one envelope of Butter Buds. One Tablespoon of dry Butter Buds Sprinkle is the same as one packet of dry Butter Buds. Butter Buds 1-800-231-1123.

Here's to good eatin'
(without any guilt! ☺)
So enjoy! And God Bless!
Love,
Dawn

Section 1
Recipes That Can Be Made Quickly and Effortlessly

Appetizers
Snacks
Beverages

Appetizers, Snacks, Beverages

♥ *"Seconds Please" Mexican Dip* ♥

Serves 15

1.43 Fat Grams (not including chips)

Prep Time: 10 minutes

Calories: 87

It doesn't get any easier (or tastier) than this! Eat as a meal or appetizer.

1 **pound ground eye of round beef**
1 **8-ounce package no-fat Mexican cheese**
(I use Healthy Choice)
1 **16-ounce jar of mild thick 'n chunky picante or thick chunky salsa**
(I use Old El Paso picante)
1 **16-ounce can vegetarian refried beans**
(I use Old El Paso)

In large pan brown beef. Do not drain juice. Add cheese, picante, and refried beans. Stir until well mixed and hot. Keep warm in a Crock-Pot. Serve warm with low-fat tortilla chips! MMM! MMM! GOOD!

♥ *Italian Dip* ♥

♥

Serves 19

.5 Fat Grams

Prep Time: 3 minutes

Calories: 56

My husband, who doesn't like to cook, came up with this version himself. Jokingly he told me, "Your creations are becoming contagious! You've even got me doing it now!"

14 **ounces Ragu Pizza Sauce**
(We like garlic and basil flavor)
16 **ounces fat-free sour cream**
8 **ounces fancy shredded mozzarella cheese**
(We like Healthy Choice)

Mix together. Serve chilled. Great for baked Tostitos or pretzels.

Kids Cookin'

♥ *Mexican Confetti Dip* ♥

This is a great source of protein. I like to eat this for lunch.

1   **12-ounce can whole kernel corn, drained**
1   **15.5-ounce can black beans, drained**
⅓   **cup fat-free Italian salad dressing**
     (I use Marzetti)
1   **16-ounce jar of your favorite chunky salsa**

Mix all together. Chill. Presto! You're done! Serve with Baked Tostito Chips.

Other ways to use this recipe:

Warm a flour tortilla in microwave. Fill center with ¼ cup of dip. Fold up as you would a burrito.

Toss ½ cup with 1½ cup of your favorite lettuces for a tasty twist to your salad!

Serves 6

.75 Fat Grams

Prep Time:
5 minutes

Calories: 78

Kids Cookin'

♥ *South of the Border Cheese Spread* ♥

8   **ounces fat-free cream cheese, softened**
16   **ounces fat-free sour cream**
1   **16-ounce jar of your favorite salsa**
16   **ounces fat-free shredded cheddar or**
     taco cheese

With blender, mix ingredients thoroughly. Serve chilled with crackers (I like SnackWell's fat-free brand) or low-fat tortilla chips.

♥

Serves 28

0 Fat Grams

Prep Time:
5 minutes

Calories: 45
(without
crackers)

♥ *Fruit-flavored Cream Cheese Spreads* ♥

Serves 20

0 Fat Grams

**Prep Time:
4 minutes**

Calories: 40

Great for bagels or crackers! The high fat in those expensive so-called "lite" flavored cheese spreads got my creativity going! I'm so pleased with these! They all taste absolutely delicious and not 1 gram of fat!

2   8-ounce packages Healthy Choice fat-free cream cheese

**½   cup your favorite jam
(If it's not sweet enough, add 1 or 2 envelopes NutraSweet)**

Here are my favorite types of jam to use in this recipe:

strawberry	blackberry	blueberry
apricot	peach	raspberry

♥ *"Chili Cheeser Pleaser" Dip* ♥

Serves 15

1.06 Fat Grams

**Prep Time:
7 minutes**

**Calories: 84
(without chips)**

It's hard to believe it's only 1 gram of fat!

1   pound ground eye of round (beef)

**2   15-ounce cans fat-free Chili with black beans
(I use Health Valley spicy vegetarian)**

**8   ounces fat-free fancy shredded cheddar cheese
(I use Healthy Choice)**

Brown hamburger. Add chili and cheddar cheese. Mix well over medium-low heat until cheese is melted. Serve warm with either low-fat tortilla chips, fat-free pretzel chips, or low-fat Bugles.

♥ *No Cooking Mexican Dip* ♥

Serves 15

.1 Fat Gram

Prep Time:
15 minutes

Calories: 60
(without chips)

8　ounces fat-free cream cheese
　　(I use Healthy Choice)
8　ounces fat-free sour cream
16　ounces your favorite thick and
　　chunky salsa
　　(Picante or taco sauce may be used, if desired)
2-3　green onions, chopped
1½　cup thinly sliced lettuce
1　medium tomato, diced
8　ounces fat-free Mexican shredded
　　cheese OR fat-free shredded cheddar
　　cheese
　　(I use Healthy Choice)
　　Low-fat tortilla chips

Beat cream cheese and sour cream together. Spread on cake plate. Layer other ingredients on top of cream mixture in exact order as listed above. Serve with tortilla chips.

Some things are better given away — love, hugs, and smiles!

Serves 30

0 Fat Grams

Prep Time:
3 minutes

Calories: 10
(without chips)

♥ *Cool & Creamy Spicy Tortilla Dip* ♥

I created this recipe especially for Oprah as a gift when I was fortunate enough to be in her studio audience. (By the way, she is even more beautiful in person!) She was so kind; she even sent me a thank you note!

16 ounces fat-free sour cream
1 16-ounce jar of your favorite chunky salsa

Mix together and refrigerate. Serve with low-fat tortilla chips or any other of your favorite snacks as a dip (like low-fat Bugles).

For a heartier dip add 8 ounces fancy shredded fat-free cheddar cheese. (I like Healthy Choice.) If you like spicier foods, feel free to add a few drops of Tabasco sauce. I like to use a chunky salsa rather than a regular salsa.

Serves 34

0 Fat Grams

Prep Time:
4 minutes

Calories: 10

♥ *Cool & Creamy Salsa Salad Dressing* ♥

16 ounces fat-free sour cream
1 16-ounce jar of your favorite salsa or taco sauce
⅓-½ cup skim milk
Tabasco sauce to taste (if desired)

Mix all ingredients well. Serve chilled. Keep unused portions refrigerated.

If you like a thinner-runnier salad dressing, just add more skim milk.

♥ *Fat-free Vegetable Dip* ♥

Serves 8

0 Fat Grams

Prep Time:
7 minutes

With Equal —
Calories: 35
With sugar —
Calories: 39

¾   **cup non-fat cottage cheese**
1   **package reduced calorie ranch dressing mix**
      (I use Hidden Valley)
1   **packet Equal** (OR 2 teaspoons sugar)
4   **ounces fat-free cream cheese**
¾   **cup non-fat sour cream**
3   **Tablespoons water**

Beat cottage cheese on high for 1-2 minutes (until smooth and creamy). Add everything else. Beat on medium until well blended.

♥ *Creamy Blue Cheese Salad Dressing* ♥

♥
Serves 40

.4 Grams Fat

Prep Time:
8 minutes

Calories: 16

If you like blue cheese, you'll love this!!

¼   **cup skim milk**
1   **cup fat-free sour cream**
      (I use Land O Lakes)
1   **cup fat-free mayonnaise**
      (I use Kraft free)
¼   **cup blue cheese**
      (I use Sargento's, natural crumbled)

Mix and cover. Refrigerate for at least 24 hours before using. The refrigeration time allows for the cheese to flavor the dressing.

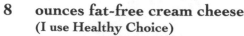

♥ *Ham & Cheese Spread* ♥

Serves 32

.62 Fat Grams

**Prep Time:
10 minutes**

**Calories: 18
(without
crackers)**

8   **ounces fat-free cream cheese**
       (I use Healthy Choice)
½   **medium red onion** (about ½ cup)
2   **6-ounce packages deli-thin sliced ham**

Put all ingredients in food processor at once. Keep on for about 35 to 45 seconds. Put into container and place in the middle of fat-free crackers. Make ahead and keep refrigerated. Don't put fat-free crackers around dip until ready to serve.

♥ *Shrimp Cocktail Spread* ♥

♥

Serves 12

.41 Fat Grams

**Prep Time:
5 minutes**

**Calories: 59
(without
crackers)**

1½   **cups frozen salad shrimp**
8   **ounces fat-free cream cheese**
       (I use Kraft Philadelphia Free)
1   **cup cocktail sauce**
       (Use your favorite or make your own with ketchup
       and horseradish)
1   **box of your favorite fat-free crackers**
       (I like SnackWell's and Health Valley)

Cook shrimp as directed on package and drain. Set aside. Spread cream cheese on 12-inch serving or cake plate, leaving ½-inch space around rim of plate. Cover the bottom of the plate completely. Spread cocktail sauce over cream cheese. Place shrimp on top of cocktail sauce. Serve with your favorite fat-free crackers.

♥ Ham & Cheese Ball ♥

Serves 12

.4 Fat Grams

Prep Time:
10 minutes

Calories: 57

4   ounces Healthy Choice ham or turkey
     ham, very thinly chopped, divided
2   8-ounce containers fat-free cream
     cheese
4   green onions, chopped
1   4-ounce can mushroom pieces, chopped
     and drained
1   Tablespoon mustard

Set ½ of the chopped ham aside. Mix all remaining
ingredients together well. Roll into a ball. Press remaining
ham onto ball, covering entire surface. Chill. Serve with
fat-free crackers. (I like SnackWell's brand.)

♥ Zesty Snack Mix ♥

♥

Serves 9

0 Fat Grams

Prep Time:
4 minutes

Calories: 126

9   cups Kellogg's Crispix cereal
1   1.1-ounce package reduced-calorie
     ranch dressing mix
     (I like Hidden Valley)
     Non-fat cooking spray

Pour Crispix cereal onto cookie sheets. Spray Crispix
cereal with a non-fat cooking spray. Sprinkle dry salad
dressing mix over cereal immediately. (The cooking spray
will hold the seasoning on the cereal.) Pour into a large
plastic bag and shake. Store at room temperature.

If this is too zesty for you, just add more Crispix cereal.

♥ *Caesar Oyster Crackers* ♥

Serves 21

1 Fat Gram

Prep Time:
4 minutes

Calories: 67

My husband loves to snack on junk food snacks! My problem with that, even though he's slender, is that he's eating loads of fat. So I try to keep as few high fat munchie type snacks around as I can. To satisfy his "Munchies Tooth," I've created some very low-fat, crunchy, and tasty snacks. I really like this one! He does, too!

11   ounces oyster crackers
1   1.2-ounce envelope gourmet Caesar salad
**   dressing mix**
**   (I like Good Seasons)**
**   Non-fat cooking spray**

Put ⅓ of the oyster crackers in either a Ziploc bag or a container with an airtight seal. Quickly spray with non-fat cooking spray. Sprinkle with ⅓ of the dry salad dressing mix. Shake well to insure good coverage of the seasonings. Repeat this process two more times.

(If you are able to buy fat-free oyster crackers, this recipe would be fat-free also.)

Life is short,
so make it
sweet.

♥ Sweet & Salty Snack Mix ♥

8 cups Ripple Crisp Honey Bran cereal
8 cups fat-free pretzels, broken up into ½-1-inch pieces.
2 cups raisins

Mix all together. Store at room temperature in airtight container. Stays crisp!

A huge hit for the kids! And healthy, too! No cooking involved. Great for kids to make and eat. You know kids always like food more when they help make it!

Serves 25

.7 Fat Grams

Prep Time: 9 minutes

Calories: 105

Kids Cookin'

♥ Barbeque Snack Mix ♥

9 cups Kellogg's Crispix cereal
1 1.9-ounce packet barbecue chicken seasoned coating microwave mix
Non-fat cooking spray

Cover cookie sheet with foil. Put 3 cups of Crispix cereal on foil. Spray with non-fat cooking spray. Sprinkle with ⅓ barbecue seasoning mix. Put into airtight container. Repeat this process until all the cereal is coated. Place cereal in an airtight container and shake the container to help cover cereal with more seasoning.

Presto!! You're done!!

♥
Serves 9

.44 Fat Grams

Prep Time: 4 minutes

Calories: 132

♥ *Chipped Beef Cheese Ball* ♥

Serves 16

.6 Fat Grams

Prep Time:
15 minutes

Calories: 45

3   8-ounce packages fat-free cream cheese
½-2 teaspoons liquid smoke
     (depending on how smoky you like it)
2   2.5-ounce packages chipped beef, chopped
     (I use Carl Budding beef)
1   small onion, chopped (approximately ½ cup)

Mix all ingredients well with blender. With hands, shape into a ball. Garnish with fresh parsley if desired. Serve with fat-free crackers.

°°°*For a quick chipped beef cheese spread* put into food processor for about 1½ to 2 minutes. Pour into bowl and garnish with crackers.

♥ *Cheese Ball* ♥

♥

Serves 18

0 Fat Grams

Prep Time:
10 minutes

Calories: 57

(Makes Two)

1   package reduced-calorie ranch dressing
     mix (I use Hidden Valley)
     cup fat-free mayonnaise (Do not use Miracle
     Whip)
½   cup skim milk
12   ounces fat-free cream cheese, softened
     (I use Healthy Choice)
1   pound fat-free fancy shredded cheddar
     cheese (I use Healthy Choice)

Mix ranch dressing with mayonnaise and milk. Mix softened cream cheese with dressing mixture until thoroughly blended. Add cheddar cheese and mix well. Form into two balls. Refrigerate 2 hours or overnight.

♥ *Cranberry Cooler (Slushy Drink)* ♥

Kids Cookin'

4-4½ cups ice
½ cup whole berry cranberry sauce
3 cups prepared cranberry breeze Crystal Light drink
4 packets Equal (or 3 Tablespoons sugar)

Put everything in blender on high, mix for 30-45 seconds. Serve immediately.

Serves 5

0 Fat Grams

Prep Time: 5 minutes

With Equal — 15 Calories
With sugar — 39 Calories

♥ *Country Raspberry Tea* ♥

Kids Cookin'

3 teaspoons instant tea
1 quart cold water
½ quart Country Raspberry 100% juice (Dole)
3 Tablespoons NutraSweet Spoonful (OR 3 Tablespoons sugar)

Mix instant tea with water. Add remaining ingredients and stir. Serve chilled.

♥

Serves 6

0 Fat Grams

Prep Time: 5 minutes

With NutraSweet— Calories: 47
With sugar — Calories: 71

♥ *Mandarin Tangerine Tea* ♥

Serves 8

0 Fat Grams

Prep Time:
5 minutes

With
NutraSweet—
Calories: 80
With sugar —
Calories: 96

3   **teaspoons instant tea**
1   **quart cold water**
1   **quart Mandarin Tangerine 100% juice** (Dole)
2   **Tablespoons NutraSweet Spoonful** (OR 2 Tablespoons sugar)

Mix instant tea with water. Add remaining ingredients and stir. Serve chilled.

♥

Serves 6

0 Fat Grams

With
NutraSweet—
Calories: 40
With sugar —
Calories: 48

♥ *Cherry Tea* ♥

These imitation-flavored teas can save you oodles of money! Save your name brand single serving size tea bottles and refill with your own homemade! Now that's recycling!

3   **teaspoons instant tea**
1   **quart water**
¹/₂   **quart Mountain Cherry 100% Juice** (Dole)
1   **Tablespoon NutraSweet Spoonful** (OR 1 Tablespoon sugar)

Add instant tea to water and mix well. Add remaining ingredients and stir. Serve chilled.

♥ *Banana Berry Slushy* ♥

1   **banana**
1   **cup black raspberries or blackberries**
½   **cup NutraSweet Spoonful**
      (OR ½ cup sugar)
3   **cups ice**
2   **cups water**
1   **envelope black cherry Kool-Aid**

Put everything in blender on high — mix for 30-45 seconds. Serve immediately.

Serves 5

.2 Fat Grams

Prep Time:
5 minutes

With
NutraSweet—
Calories: 71
With sugar —
Calories: 110

♥ *Cherry Slushies* ♥

12   **Bing cherries, seeds removed**
4   **cups ice**
½   **teaspoon cherry-flavored sugar-free Kool-Aid**
2½ **cups cold water**
½   **cup sugar or 7 - 8 packets Equal**

Put everything in blender on "mix" or "ice crush" setting. Leave on for 30-45 seconds. Pour into glasses.

Serves 5

0 Fat Grams

Prep Time:
15 minutes

Calories: 89

♥ Warm Whatcha' Macallit ♥

Serves 24

0 Fat Grams

Prep Time:
15-18 minutes

Calories: 88

1	**gallon cider**
2	**liters diet ginger ale**
½	**cup red hots** (little red cinnamon candies)
	Cinnamon sticks (optional)

Mix all ingredients in large saucepan and stir over medium heat until warm (approximately 7-10 minutes). Serve warm with cinnamon stick.

♥ Fruit Punch ♥

♥

Serves 36

0 Fat Grams

Prep Time:
5 minutes

2 cans orange juice
Calories: 14
1 can orange juice
Calories: 11

2	**2-quart cherry sugar-free Kool-Aid**
1	**2-liter diet cherry Seven-Up**
2	**12-ounce cans of frozen orange juice, prepared**

Mix and serve chilled. For a lower calorie punch, use only 1 can (12-ounce) orange juice. I like it just as well as 2 cans, and it's not as fattening.

If using a punch bowl, slice 1 orange and float slices on top of punch.

How do you want to be remembered in ten years? Live it now.

♥♥♥

♥ *Orange Slushy* ♥

4½   cups ice
½   teaspoon orange sugar-free Kool-Aid
2½   cups cold water
7-8   packets Equal (OR ⅓ cup sugar)
1   11-ounce can Mandarin oranges with
    lite syrup

Put all ingredients in blender and blend for 30-45 seconds.
Pour into glasses and serve.

Serves 5

.1 Fat Grams

Prep Time:
5 minutes

With Equal —
Calories: 37
With sugar —
Calories: 64

♥ *Peach Tea* ♥

3   teaspoons instant tea
1   quart cold water
½   quart Orchard Peach 100% juice (Dole)
2½   Tablespoons NutraSweet (OR 2½
     Tablespoons sugar)

Add tea to water and mix well. Add remaining ingredients
and stir. Serve chilled.

♥

Serves 6

0 Fat Grams

Prep Time:
5-7 minutes

With
NutraSweet—
Calories: 47
With sugar —
Calories: 67

♥ *Very Berry Tea* ♥

<table>
<tr><td>3</td><td>teaspoons instant tea</td></tr>
<tr><td>1</td><td>quart cold water</td></tr>
<tr><td>½</td><td>quart Cranberry/Strawberry Juice Cocktail Blend with Grape Juice</td></tr>
<tr><td>8</td><td>ounces Mountain Cherry 100% juice (Dole)</td></tr>
<tr><td>8</td><td>ounces Country Raspberry 100% juice (Dole)</td></tr>
<tr><td>3</td><td>Tablespoons NutraSweet Spoonful (OR 3 Tablespoons sugar)</td></tr>
</table>

Add tea to water and mix well. Add remaining ingredients and stir. Serve chilled.

Serves 8

0 Fat Grams

Prep Time:
5-7 minutes

With NutraSweet—
Calories: 47
With sugar —
Calories: 71

♥ *Hawaiian Slushy Drink* ♥

<table>
<tr><td>1</td><td>15-ounce can pineapple, in juice (not syrup)</td></tr>
<tr><td>2</td><td>bananas</td></tr>
<tr><td>⅓</td><td>cup NutraSweet Spoonful (OR ½ cup sugar)</td></tr>
<tr><td>2-2½</td><td>cups ice (depending on how icy you like it)</td></tr>
<tr><td>1</td><td>teaspoon of piña-pineapple sugar-free Kool-Aid</td></tr>
</table>

Put everything in a blender. Fill blender to top with water. Mix on high for 30-45 seconds, until slushy.

♥

Serves 6

.1 Fat Grams

Prep Time:
5-7 minutes

With NutraSweet—
Calories: 92
With sugar —
Calories: 156

♥ *Banana Smoothie* ♥

1	banana
1½	cups skim milk
5	Tablespoons NutraSweet Spoonful
	(OR 5 Tablespoons sugar)
2	cups ice

Put everything in blender on high; mix for 30-45 seconds. Serve immediately.

Serves 5

.1 Fat Grams

Prep Time:
5 minutes

With
NutraSweet—
Calories: 47
With sugar —
Calories: 93

♥ *Mint Tea* ♥

If you like Snapple mint tea, you'll love this, and it'll save you loads of money!

2	quarts hot water
8	tea bags (your favorite brand)
2	drops mint extract
	Sugar to taste (optional)

Put tea bags in hot water. Let stand overnight. Remove tea bags. Put 2 drops of mint extract into tea. Serve in tall glasses with ice.

♥

Serves 8

0 Fat Grams

Prep Time:
5 minutes

Calories: 6

A smile speaks every leanguage.

Breads
&
Rolls

Breads & Rolls

♥ *Italian Biscuits* ♥

Serves 5	

1 Fat Gram

Prep Time: 25 minutes

Calories: 105 (without butter)

1   **10-count can of Rightshape Biscuits** OR **Pillsbury Buttermilk Biscuits**
4   **Tablespoons Italian-style bread crumbs** (I use Progresso)

Preheat oven to 425 degrees. Spray cookie sheet with a non-fat spray. Gently press each biscuit into bread crumbs, covering the biscuit tops completely. With crumb side up, place biscuits on cookie sheet. Bake 20 minutes or until tops are golden brown. If desired, you can warm 1 Tablespoon Butter Buds and brush tops of biscuits once cooked. Serve warm.

♥ *Sticky Breakfast Bagels* ♥

♥

Serves 12

1.2 Fat Grams

Prep Time: 8-10 minutes

Calories: 249

8   **ounces fat-free margarine** (I use Ultra Promise)
½   **teaspoon vanilla**
1   **cup brown sugar**
2   **teaspoons cinnamon**
1   **dozen bagels, cut in half**

Put margarine, vanilla, brown sugar, and cinnamon into blender and blend on medium speed for 1 minute. Take bagel halves and dip top with spread just prepared. If needed, spread with knife. Broil for 4 to 5 minutes, or until bubbly and brown. Serve warm.

♥ *Garlic Crisp* ♥

Pita bread (I use Father Sam's large size)
Non-fat cooking spray
Garlic salt
**Grated Italian topping or grated
Parmesan cheese, approximately
1 Tablespoon per pita**
Dried basil

Preheat oven to 350 degrees. Cut each pita into 8 equal pieces. Spray bread pieces with non-fat spray. Sprinkle with garlic salt, grated Italian topping (or Parmesan cheese) and basil, in that order. Bake for 10 minutes or until slightly brown on edges. Great warm or serve later with salad instead of croutons.

♥ *Cheesy Vegetable Bread* ♥

1	**teaspoon garlic salt**
1	**teaspoon dried basil**
1	**teaspoon dried parsley**
½	**cup liquid Butter Buds**
1	**loaf vegetable bread, sliced into ¾-inch slices** (find in deli area)
2	**Tablespoons Molly McButter Cheese Sprinkles**
¼	**cup Parmesan cheese**

Spray cookie sheet with a non-fat spray. Add garlic salt, dried basil, and dried parsley to liquid Butter Buds. Spread liquid Butter Buds over bread slices. Place slices of bread on prepared cookie sheet. Sprinkle with cheese sprinkles and Parmesan cheese. Broil until tops are browned and toasty. Serve warm. MMM!

Soups
Salads
Vegetables

Soups, Salads, Vegetables

Serves 20

1.8 Fat Grams

Prep Time:
30 minutes

Calories: 116

♥ *Chicken Asparagus Soup* ♥

12   **cups chicken broth**
6   **chicken breasts** (skinless, boneless, with fat removed)
1   **teaspoon Cajun seasoning**
3   **bay leaves**
1   **4.5-ounce package Staff Cheddar Broccoli Rice & Sauce mix**
1   **15-ounce can asparagus, cut into pieces**
1   **teaspoon parsley**
    Salt to taste (optional)

Bring chicken broth to a rapid boil. Add all ingredients, and bring to a rapid boil again. Reduce heat to a low boil. Boil 10 minutes. Remove breasts and chop into bite-sized pieces. Put cut-up breast pieces back into soup. Serve warm. Remove bay leaves before eating.

♥ *Vegetable Hobo Soup* ♥

Serves 11

.8 Fat Grams

Prep Time:
20 minutes

Calories: 104

I like to serve this vegetarian soup with warm vegetable bread.

3   **pounds frozen mixed vegetables**
1   **46-ounce can V-8 Vegetable Juice**
2   **bay leaves**
    Salt to taste
    Garlic powder to taste

Put all ingredients in a large soup pan or Dutch Oven. Bring to a boil. Reduce heat. Cook 15 minutes. Serve hot.

Kids Cookin'

♥ *Creamy Cucumbers* ♥

Serves 14

.1 Fat Grams

Prep Time:
15 minutes

Calories: 57

3   large cucumbers, peeled and thinly sliced
1   medium onion, thinly sliced
1   16-ounce bottle fat-free ranch salad dressing (I use Marzetti's)

Toss all ingredients and chill. Serve chilled.

Kids Cookin'

♥ *Tomato Zing Salad* ♥

♥
Serves 12

.2 Fat Grams

Prep Time:
10-15 minutes

Calories: 17

1   package no-fat Italian dressing (I use Seven Seas)
     Rice vinegar
2   large cucumbers, peeled and thinly sliced
1   pint cherry tomatoes
1   medium onion, chopped

Mix dressing with rice vinegar, according to package directions. Toss vegetables in dressing. Serve chilled.

Kids Cookin'

♥ *Creamy Zucchini & Squash Salad* ♥

Serves 5

.1 Fat Grams

Prep Time:
15 minutes

Calories: 51

2   10-inch zucchini, peeled and thinly sliced
2   10-inch yellow squash, peeled and thinly sliced
1   medium onion, thinly sliced
16   ounces fat-free ranch salad dressing (I use Marzetti's)

Toss vegetables in dressing. Serve chilled.

♥ *Red-Wine Vinaigrette Cucumber Salad* ♥

Kids Cookin'

A summer must! Great for cookouts! My children and I like to nibble on these for a snack.

4 - 5 cucumbers, peeled and sliced into ¼-inch slices

16 ounces Seven Seas Red-Wine Vinaigrette Salad Dressing

Toss cucumber slices in the dressing. Serve chilled.

♥ *Papa Pasta Salad* ♥

16 ounces Rotini pasta

8 ounces uncooked smoked sausage, cut into tiny pieces
(I use Healthy Choice)

1 Tablespoon + 1 teaspoon Durkee Salad Seasoning

1½ cups fat-free ranch dressing
(I use Henri's brand)

Cook Rotini pasta as directed. Drain. Rinse with cold water until pasta is cool. Drain. Add remaining ingredients. Serve chilled.

♥ *Summer Fiesta! Salad* ♥

Serves 4

.4 Fat Grams

Prep Time:
25-30 minutes

Calories: 106
(without
dressing)

For a faster salad, use prepared, cut-up salad greens (lettuce).

½   **pound cooked chicken breasts or chicken breast lunch meat sliced into ¼-inch strips**

1   **small onion, chopped**
(red onion is best, but any one will do)

4   **small hard-boiled egg whites**

6   **cups of your favorite lettuces, torn into bite-sized pieces.**
(Iceberg, spinach, and leaf are my favorites)

1   **small carrot, diced**

1   **medium tomato, cut into bite-sized pieces**
Fat-free honey Dijon salad dressing

Toss ingredients in salad dressing.

Kids Cookin'

♥ *Hot — Not Fat — Fruit Salad* ♥

This is a soupy salad and needs to be served in a bowl. I like it as a dessert over frozen vanilla yogurt.

Serves 30

.2 Fat Grams

Prep Time:
20 minutes

Calories: 69

1   **20-ounce can pineapple**

1   **20-ounce can pears**

1   **20-ounce can peaches**

1   **20-ounce can apricots**

1   **20-ounce can lite cherry pie filling**

¾   **cup brown sugar**

1   **pound fat-free margarine**
(I use Ultra Promise)

Drain fruit for at least 1 hour. Preheat oven to 350 degrees. Mix brown sugar, margarine, fruit and pie filling together. Bake for 1 hour (or microwave on high till warm, about 5 minutes).

Note: If desired, you can put all ingredients in a Crock-Pot on low and let it simmer all day.

♥ *Fresh Broccoli Salad* ♥

Serves 4

Prep Time:
5 minutes

⅓ cup Free Miracle Whip

⅓ cup Fat-free Catalina dressing (OR Fat-free Western dressing)

1 large head fresh broccoli, cut into bite-sized pieces.

Combine Miracle Whip and dressing. Mix well. Pour dressing over broccoli. Stir until well coated with dressing. Serve chilled.

♥ *Apple Salad* ♥

♥

Serves 16
.2 Fat Grams

Prep Time:
15 minutes

With
NutraSweet—
Calories: 71
With sugar —
Calories: 95

1½ cups non-fat cottage cheese

¾ cup fat-free mayonnaise

¾ teaspoon cinnamon

½ cup NutraSweet Spoonful (OR ½ cup sugar)

4 cups finely chopped apples (approximately 4-5 large apples)

¼ cup raisins, finely chopped

3 bananas, sliced diagonally

In blender, whip cottage cheese, mayonnaise, cinnamon, and NutraSweet until cottage cheese is smooth and creamy (about 3 to 4 minutes). Pour into medium bowl and mix in apples, raisins, and sliced bananas. Presto! It's ready to eat!

♥ *Chicken Salad* ♥

Serves 3

2 Fat Grams

Prep Time:
5 minutes

Calories: 56

Great for sandwiches on toasted lite bread or stuffing in cherry tomatoes as appetizers!

- **2   teaspoons sweet relish**
- **3   teaspoons fat-free mayonnaise**
  (I use Kraft)
- **1   6-ounce package Oscar Mayer deli-thin**
  roasted chicken breast, cut into 1-inch
  pieces

Mix all ingredients in blender for about 30 seconds. It doesn't get any easier than this!

♥ *Apple Yam Casserole* ♥

Serves 12

.1 Grams Fat

Prep Time:
25 minutes

Calories: 121

This is a great dish for holidays.

- **1   20-ounce can apple pie filling**
- **½   teaspoon cinnamon**
- **2   Tablespoons brown sugar**
  Dash of salt (optional)
- **1   24-ounce can yams, drained and cut**
  into bite-sized pieces

Cut apples in pie filling into bite-sized pieces. In a medium bowl mix apple pie filling, cinnamon, brown sugar, and salt until well blended. Gently stir in cut-up yams. Spray two-quart casserole dish with non-fat cooking spray. Pour in mixture, and microwave until warm about 5 minutes, stirring occasionally. Serve warm.

♥ *Seasoned Rice* ♥

This dish is excellent with the "Oriental Teriyaki Beef Dinner."

1   **cup long grain rice**
2¼   **cups water**
1   **1.4-ounce envelope Knorr vegetable soup mix**

Spray medium saucepan with a non-fat cooking spray. Add all ingredients, stir and dissolve soup. Bring to a boil, then reduce heat to simmering. Cover and cook approximately 20 minutes.

♥ *Oniony Chicken Rice Dish* ♥

1   **pound chicken breasts, skinless, boneless, and cut into bite-sized pieces**
1   **14.5-ounce can chicken broth** (remove any floating fat)
2   **cups frozen green beans**
1   **cup natural long grain rice**
¼   **cup fat-free margarine** (I use Ultra Promise)
1   **1.5-ounce package dry onion soup mix**
⅓   **cup water**

Spray Dutch Oven with a non-fat cooking spray. Combine all ingredients in the Dutch Oven and cook over medium heat. Bring to a boil, then reduce to simmer for 23 minutes covered. Stir occasionally. Turn off heat and let stand for five minutes before serving.

♥ *Green Bean Delite* ♥

1   medium onion, chopped
8   ounces mushrooms, thinly sliced
½   cup liquid Butter Buds
8   ounces lean ham, diced
3   15.5-ounce cans French-style green
      beans, drained
3   Tablespoons honey
1   teaspoon lite salt (optional)

Sauté onions and mushrooms in Butter Buds until tender.
Add ham, green beans, and honey. Cook over medium heat
until heated thoroughly. Add salt if desired.

Serves 15

.9 Fat Grams

Prep Time:
20 minutes

Calories: 55

♥ *Almost Homemade Dressing* ♥

The slight crunchiness of the corn mixed with the turkey, onion,
mushrooms, and seasoning makes this taste homemade — to be honest —
just as good as my homemade!

3⅓   cups water plus ½ cup
1   medium onion, chopped
2   4-ounce cans sliced mushrooms
1   package Butter Buds — dry — OR
      1 Tablespoon Butter Buds Sprinkles
1   16-ounce can corn
2   boxes chicken stuffing (I use Stove Top)
2   cups chopped turkey or chicken breast
⅛   teaspoon ground pepper

Put water, chopped onion, mushrooms, Butter Buds, and
seasoning packets from stuffing mixes into medium
saucepan. Bring to a boil. Reduce heat. Add corn. Simmer 4
minutes. Add bread crumbs from stuffing boxes. Remove
from heat. Let sit 5 minutes. Heat turkey in microwave until warm
(about 40 seconds). Season turkey with pepper. Stir turkey into
stuffing. Serve immediately.

Serves 15

.9 Fat Grams

Prep Time:
20 minutes

Calories: 55

♥ *Mama's Beans* ♥

If you like green beans with ham, you'll like this!

16 **ounces frozen cut green beans**
⅓ **cup fat-free fancy shredded mozzarella cheese** (I use Healthy Choice)
4 **slices hardwood smoked white turkey lunch meat, cut into tiny pieces**
1 **Tablespoon grated Parmesan cheese Dash of pepper** (optional)
1 **teaspoon fat-free garlic butter sprinkles, optional** (I use Molly McButter)

Mix green beans, mozzarella, turkey, and Parmesan cheese. Add seasonings if desired. Microwave 6 to 8 minutes, stirring occasionally. Serve as a side dish or eat as a main meal. Dish is completely cooked when beans are hot, crisp yet tender, and cheese is melted.

♥ *Potatoes A-La-Larry* ♥

This delicious recipe is from a friend named Larry, who is an excellent cook for the Cherry Street Mission here in Toledo, Ohio. This recipe tastes so good, it can fool some folks into thinking they're made from scratch! Just between you and me, "Don't tell them they aren't unless they ask!" It'll be our little secret!

Chicken broth (from a can, preferably)
Instant mashed potatoes
Skim milk
Fat-free margarine (I use Fleishmann's)
1 **15-20-ounce can potatoes, drained and mashed**
¼ **cup fresh onion, finely chopped** (per every 8 servings)

Substituting chicken broth for water, use exact same measurements needed to prepare instant mashed potatoes, according to package directions. Stir in milk, margarine, mashed potatoes, and onion. Presto!! You're done.

♥ *Quick Asparagus Casserole* ♥

This is a nice variety to take to a potluck.

Serves 12

.8 Fat Grams

Prep Time:
20 minutes

Calories: 100

1   **14.5-ounce can asparagus, drained**
2   **cups non-fat buttermilk (skim milk can be substituted if desired)**
1   **envelope Butter Buds — dry**
2   **Tablespoons flour**
½   **cup light mozzarella cheese shredded (I use Sargento Light)**
½   **cup Italian bread crumbs (I use Progresso brand; if you don't like the zest of the Italian, you can use plain)**

Preheat oven to 350 degrees. Spray a 9 x 13-inch pan with a non-fat cooking spray. Spread asparagus evenly in the pan. Set aside. In medium saucepan, warm milk, Butter Buds, and flour on low heat. Cook about 3 minutes, stirring constantly until thickened. Add cheese and cook slowly on low heat 1 more minute. Pour sauce evenly over asparagus. Sprinkle bread crumbs over entire dish. Bake for 15 to 20 minutes, until hot and bubbly. Let cool a few minutes before serving.

♥ *Buttered Collard Greens With Ham* ♥

Serves 6

1.16 Fat Grams

Prep Time:
25 minutes

Calories: 60

2   **15-ounce cans chopped collard greens**
1   **apple, quartered, with seeds removed**
1   **Tablespoon Butter Buds**
6   **ounces deli-thin sliced boiled ham, cut into bite-sized pieces (I use deli-thin Oscar Mayer boiled ham)**
1   **small onion, chopped (approximately 1/3 cup)**

Drain collard greens. In large saucepan, combine all ingredients, and cook over medium heat. Cover and bring to a boil. Reduce heat to low. Simmer covered for 10 minutes. Remove apple quarters before serving.

Main Dishes

&

Casseroles

Main Dishes &
Casseroles

Serves 6

2.2 Fat Grams

Prep Time:
30 minutes

Calories: 197

♥ *Delicious Chicken Roll-ups* ♥

2	cups hot water
1	package Butter Buds — dry
¾	cup chopped mushrooms
1	package stuffing mix
	(I use Stove Top)
1	16-ounce package roasted chicken breast lunch meat slices

In microwave saucepan, combine hot water, Butter Buds, mushrooms, and seasoning packet from stuffing mix. Microwave on high for 2½ to 3 minutes. Add stuffing. Mix well. Cover tightly and let stand for 5 minutes. Take each chicken breast lunch meat slice and press about 2 Tablespoons of stuffing mix in middle of lunch meat slice. Bring sides of slice into middle and secure with toothpick.

Preheat oven to 350 degrees. Lay chicken rolls on jelly roll pan (cookie sheet with edges) that has been sprayed with a non-fat cooking spray. Pour sauce (recipe follows) over tops of each roll, allowing sauce to cover bottom of pan. Cover with foil. Bake for 15 minutes.

Sauce:

½	cup milk
2	Tablespoons cornstarch
1	teaspoon garlic salt
½	teaspoon Jumbalaya Cajun Seasoning (optional)
1	can chicken broth

Heat broth. Mix remaining ingredients together and add to broth. Heat until warm.

♥ *Marinated Grilled Chicken Breasts* ♥

This is delicious served with Rice-a-Roni with Almonds. Make as directed on Rice-a-Roni package except substitute 2 Tablespoon liquid Butter Buds for margarine. Use orange slice for garnish.

16   **ounces fat-free Italian dressing**
      (I like Kraft)

4   **chicken breasts, boneless, skinless, with all fat trimmed off**

Marinate raw chicken breasts in dressing for at least 1 hour, turning over once. (Overnight is best.)

Remove chicken from salad dressing. Grill or cook in covered pan that has been sprayed with non-fat spray. Cook 5 to 7 minutes until there is no pink in chicken.

Serves 4

4 Fat Grams

Prep Time:
15-20 minutes

Calories: 198

♥ *Beef-N-Noodles* ♥

This is very good served with Potatoes A-La-Larry.

1   **12-ounce jar of Heinz Fat-free Seasoned Pork OR Beef Gravy**

2   **cups pasta, cooked**

2   **cups eye of round** (beef), **cooked and shredded** (OR 1 pound Healthy Choice hamburger, browned)

Mix gravy with cooked pasta and beef. Heat and serve.

Note: Leftover spaghetti noodles will work if you have them. Just soak the cooked spaghetti completely in a bowl of water in the refrigerator until you need them for this recipe.

♥

Serves 4

6.2 Fat Grams

Prep Time:
25 minutes

Calories: 341

♥ *Southern Style Chicken Gravy Over Biscuits* ♥

1   **cup skim milk**
¼   **cup cornstarch**
1   **Tablespoon garlic salt** (optional)
1   **14.5-ounce can chicken broth** (I use Campbell's)
     Dash of pepper (optional)
3   **8-ounce cans of no salt mixed vegetables, drained**
1½   **pounds skinless chicken breasts, fully cooked and chopped into bite-sized pieces**

Put first 5 ingredients into Dutch Oven. Mix well before turning on heat, dissolving cornstarch completely. Turn heat on medium. Add drained vegetables and cooked bite-sized pieces of chicken. Stir occasionally and cook for approximately 10 to 12 minutes, until thick and creamy.°

° Serve ½ cup over 2 biscuits (I use Pillsbury Buttermilk Biscuits — 150 calories and 2 grams of fat for 3 biscuits OR Kroger Buttermilk Biscuits — 100 calories and 1.5 grams of fat for 2 biscuits)

♥ *Hamburger Gravy Over Biscuits* ♥

1   **pound ground eye of round** (beef)
1   **packet Butter Buds, dry**
2   **teaspoons garlic salt** (optional)
     Dash of pepper (optional)
3   **cups skim milk**
½   **cup cornstarch**

In a large pan or Dutch Oven cook ground eye of round, Butter Buds, pepper and garlic salt on medium heat, until meat is fully cooked. Add 2 cups skim milk. Mix cornstarch to remaining 1 cup skim milk, stirring until cornstarch is completely dissolved. Pour into beef, stirring constantly. Cook approximately 5 minutes longer, until thick and creamy.°

♥ *Chicken Noodle Casserole* ♥

Serves 9

2.5 Fat Grams

Prep Time:
40 minutes

Calories: 309

1   12-ounce bag "No Yolk" noodles
8   ounces fat-free shredded cheddar
       cheese, divided
       (I use Healthy Choice)
4   ounces mushrooms, drained
1   pound cooked chicken breasts cut into
       bite-sized pieces
3   jars chicken-flavored gravy
       (I use Heinz Homestyle)
1   teaspoon garlic salt (optional)
16   ounces mixed vegetables, drained
       Dash of pepper (optional)
2   cups crushed low-fat potato chips
       (optional, found in low-fat chip aisle)
       Parmesan cheese (optional)

Preheat oven to 350 degrees. Spray a 9 x 13-inch pan with a non-fat cooking spray. Set aside. Cook noodles as directed on package. Combine noodles with ½ of the cheese and add remaining ingredients. Pour into pan. Sprinkle remaining 4 ounces of cheese and chips on top of casserole. Bake for 20 minutes until completely warmed.

Serve with grated Parmesan cheese on the side.

Thin may be in, but fit — not fat — is where it's at!

♥♥♥

♥ *Breakfast Sandwich* ♥

Serves 1

1 Fat Gram

Prep Time:
25 minutes

Calories: 190

2　egg whites
1　**Aunt Millie's Lite fat-free Potato Hamburger Bun**
3　**slices thin-sliced ham**
　　(I use Hillshire Farm Deli Select — 10 calories per slice)
1　**slice fat-free cheddar cheese**
　　(I use Kraft Free)
　　Pepper to taste, if desired

Spray griddle and a biscuit cutter with non-fat cooking spray. Beat egg whites. Put biscuit cutter onto griddle. Pour eggs into biscuit cutter. Spray insides of hamburger buns with non-fat cooking spray and brown the buns on griddle. Warm ham slices on griddle. Cut cheese slice in half and lay on top of ham slices being warmed on the griddle. Once everything is cooked, lay ham slices with cheese on bottom part of the browned hamburger bun. Lay cooked egg on top of ham and cheese. Sprinkle with pepper, if desired. Put top of hamburger bun on bottom, and presto! Breakfast!! (Some people like mustard on this sandwich.)

♥ *Beef Stroganoff* ♥

This meal is delicious with warm bread. I like to warm French bread in the oven. People love to dip their warm French bread into the juices of the Beef Stroganoff on their plates.

2	**pounds partially frozen eye of round** (beef), **thinly sliced**
1	**large onion, thinly sliced**
8	**ounces fresh mushrooms, thinly sliced**
½	**cup liquid Butter Buds**
1	**teaspoon garlic salt**
16	**ounces non-fat sour cream**
	Pepper to taste
12	**ounces "No Yolk" noodles, cooked and drained**

Serves 8

5.9 Fat Grams

Prep Time:
40 minutes

Calories: 361

Eliminate all visible fat from meat and brown in large pan. Rinse beef under water. Set aside. Combine onion, mushrooms and liquid Butter Buds, and sauté until soft. Add cooked beef, garlic salt, sour cream, and pepper. Stir until well combined. Do *NOT* boil. Serve hot over warm noodles.

Kids Cookin'

♥ *Chili Mac* ♥

Great with corn bread.

1	**pound macaroni**
	(I like to use shell shaped)
1	**pound ground eye of round** (beef)
1	**15-ounce can Health Valley Fat-free Spicy Vegetarian Chili With Black Beans**

♥

Serves 10

2.9 Fat Grams

Prep Time:
30 minutes

Calories: 257

Cook macaroni as directed on box. Brown eye of round. Stir together chili, meat, and macaroni. Serve warm!

Serves 10

4.6 Fat Grams

Prep Time:
30 minutes

Calories: 260

♥ *Beefy-Chili Burritos With Cheese* ♥

My kids love to roll these up themselves.

1 **pound ground eye of round** (beef)
2 **cans Health Valley fat-free chili** (15-ounce spicy vegetarian with black beans)
16 **ounces fat-free fancy shredded cheddar cheese**
    (I use Healthy Choice)
1 **package fat-free flour tortilla shells**

In medium pan brown ground eye of round. Add chili and 6 ounces of cheddar cheese. Stir over medium low heat until cheese is completely dissolved (about 5 minutes). Put 1/10 of the chili mixture in the middle of a tortilla. Roll up. Sprinkle 1 ounce shredded cheddar cheese on top. Microwave about 10 to 15 seconds to melt cheese. Serve warm.

Note: Garnish with your favorite salsa if desired. With a side tossed salad and fat-free Western salad dressing, this is a complete, delicious and nutritious meal! Not included in calorie or fat information.

Serves 8

0 Fat Grams

Prep Time:
5 minutes

Calories: 185

♥ *South of the Border Hot Dogs* ♥ Kids Cookin'

A Mexican twist to an all-American food.

1 **package 8 fat-free hot dogs**
    (I use Oscar Mayer)
1 **package fat-free hot dog buns**
    (I use Aunt Millie's)
8 **Tablespoons grated fat-free cheddar cheese**
8 **Tablespoons chunky salsa**

Put one hot dog in each bun. Top with 1 Tablespoon grated cheddar cheese and 1 Tablespoon salsa. Microwave each on high for approximately 45 seconds to 1 minute. Enjoy!!

♥ *Beef Fajitas* ♥

1   **pound cooked shredded beef or Healthy Choice ground beef**
½   **cup fat-free Italian salad dressing**
10   **soft flour taco shells** (Buena Vista is fat-free)
1   **cup shredded iceberg lettuce**
1   **cup chopped tomato**
     Fat-free taco or cheddar cheese
     Fat-free sour cream (optional)

Marinate beef in dressing. Warm beef in microwave with dressing. Microwave soft taco shell until warm. Put desired amount of marinated beef on soft shell. Top with lettuce, tomato, cheese, and sour cream, if desired.

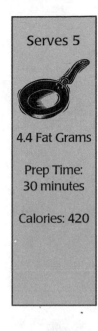

Serves 5

4.4 Fat Grams

Prep Time:
30 minutes

Calories: 420

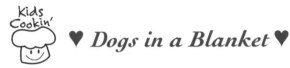

Kids Cookin'

♥ *Dogs in a Blanket* ♥

Fast, easy and fun for kids to make.

8   **Healthy Choice hot dogs**
2   **cans Pillsbury Buttermilk Biscuits**
     (4 biscuits will be left over)

Preheat oven to 350 degrees. Take 2 biscuits and wrap around a hot dog. Pinch biscuit dough with fingers to seal the "blanket." Spray 2 cookie sheets with a non-fat cooking spray. Lay 4 prepared "dogs" on each cookie sheet, making sure they are 2 to 3 inches apart, because the dough will get bigger as they cook. Bake for 10 minutes or until dough is golden brown. Serve with mustard, ketchup or barbeque sauce on the side for dipping.

♥

Serves 8

2 Fat Grams

Prep Time:
20 minutes

Calories: 150

♥ *Cheesy Dogs in a Blanket* ♥

4   slices fat-free cheese

Follow "Dogs in a Blanket" recipe exactly, except cut hot dogs ½ way through lengthwise to make just enough room for ½ slice of cheese before wrapping and baking.

♥ *Dogs on a Stick* ♥

Fast, easy and fun for kids to make.

8   Oscar Mayer fat-free hot dogs
2   cans Pillsbury Buttermilk Biscuits
       (4 biscuits will be left over)
8   popsicle sticks
       Cornmeal (optional)

Preheat oven to 350 degrees. Take 2 biscuits and wrap around hot dog, pinching biscuit dough with fingers to seal the dough around the hot dogs. Place 1 popsicle stick ½ way through each hot dog, leaving ½ of the stick out to later use as a handle. Spray 2 cookie sheets with non-fat cooking spray. Arrange "dogs" on cookie sheets, making sure they are at least 2 to 3 inches apart, because the dough will get bigger as they cook and you don't want them to stick to each other. Sprinkle with cornmeal if desired, before baking. Bake for 10 minutes or until dough is golden brown. Serve with mustard or ketchup.

♥ *Pigs on a Stick* ♥

14 ounces Healthy Choice smoked sausage
2 cans Pillsbury Buttermilk Biscuits
(4 biscuits will be left over)
8 popsicle sticks

Preheat oven to 350 degrees. Cut smoked sausage into 8 pieces. It will look like short, fat little hot dogs. Wrap each little sausage with two biscuits. Pinch biscuit dough with fingers to seal the "blanket." Place 1 popsicle stick ½ way through each sausage, leaving ½ of the stick out to later use as a handle. Spray 2 cookie sheets with non-fat cooking spray. Arrange "pigs" on cookie sheets, making sure they are at least 2 to 3 inches apart, because the dough will get bigger as they cook and you don't want them to stick to each other. Bake for 10 minutes or until dough is golden brown. Serve with mustard, ketchup, or barbeque sauce for dipping.

Serves 8

4.1 Fat Grams

Prep Time:
25 minutes

Calories: 161

 ♥ *Pigs in a Blanket* ♥

Fast, easy and fun for kids to make.

14 ounces Healthy Choice smoked sausage
2 cans Pillsbury Buttermilk Biscuits
(4 biscuits will be left over)

Preheat oven to 350 degrees. Cut smoked sausage into 8 pieces. It will look like short, fat little hot dogs. Wrap each little sausage with two biscuits. Pinch biscuit dough with fingers to seal the "blanket." Spray two cookie sheets with a non-fat spray. Arrange "Pigs" on cookie sheets, making sure they are at least 2 to 3 inches apart, because the dough will get bigger as they cook and you don't want them to stick to each other. Bake for 10 minutes or until dough is golden brown. Serve with mustard, ketchup, or barbeque sauce for dipping.

♥

Serves 8

4.1 Fat Grams

Prep Time:
20 minutes

Calories: 161

Without the Down Home Fat ♥ **73**

♥ *Cherry Breakfast Sandwich* ♥

Kids Cookin

A meal in itself! Looks like a sandwich, but eat it with a fork.

2   Special K fat-free waffles
½   cup lite cherry pie filling (warm in the
          microwave, if desired)
1   Tablespoon "lite" blueberry syrup

Toast waffles until golden brown. Spread cherry pie filling
on top of one waffle. Put second waffle on top of cherries.
Drizzle syrup over top of second waffle, allowing syrup to
run over the edges. Serve immediately.

♥

Serves 6

2 Grams Fat

Prep Time:
35 minutes

Calories: 200

♥ *Baked French Toast* ♥

What's great about this recipe is it can be prepared in advance and kept
in the refrigerator, if desired, before baking.

12   slices raisin bread
1   cup skim milk
8   egg whites
¼   cup packed brown sugar
1   teaspoon vanilla
          Powdered sugar (optional)
          Syrup (optional)

Preheat oven to 325 degrees. Spray a jelly roll pan (a
cookie sheet with ½-inch sides) with a non-fat cooking
spray. Lay 12 slices of raisin bread in three rows of four
(sides of bread will be touching). If bread is slightly stale or
dry, that's fine. Beat milk, egg whites, brown sugar, and
vanilla with mixer on high for 1½ to 2 minutes. Pour
mixture over slices of bread. Once bread is covered, turn each slice
over to guarantee all bread is wet. Bake for 27 to 30 minutes. Serve
immediately. Sprinkle powdered sugar lightly on top or syrup if
desired.

♥ *Sausage Skillet Dinner* ♥

A complete meal in itself that is fast, easy and delicious.

Serves 6

.9 Fat Grams

Prep Time:
25 minutes

Calories: 180

4   **medium potatoes**
1   **14- to 16-ounce low fat smoked sausage,
     cut into bite-sized pieces**
     (I use Healthy Choice)
1   **medium onion, chopped**
1   **packet Butter Buds, dry**
2   **15.5-ounce cans French style green
     beans with juice**
1   **teaspoon garlic salt** (optional)
     Dash of pepper (optional)

Cook potatoes in microwave until done (about 5 to 10
minutes). As the potatoes cook, spray the bottom of large
skillet with a non-fat cooking spray. Brown sausage. Add onion,
Butter Buds, green beans, garlic salt, and pepper. Cover and sauté
for 5 minutes. When the potatoes are done, cut them into bite-sized
pieces. Toss with the rest of the food in the skillet. Cover and let
simmer about 5 more minutes.

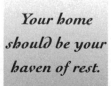

*Your home
should be your
haven of rest.*

Without the Down Home Fat ♥   **75**

♥ *Pizza Pasta* ♥

Serves 8

2.5 Fat Grams

Prep Time:
20 minutes

Calories: 203

2   **7.25-ounce boxes macaroni and cheese mix**
1   **envelope Butter Buds, dry**
1   **cup skim milk**
1   **14-ounce jar Prego Pizza Sauce with**
    Ground Sausage
8   **ounces fat-free shredded cheese, if desired**

Prepare macaroni and cheese as directed on box, substituting dry Butter Buds for butter and skim milk for ½ cup milk. Once cheese is well mixed in, add pizza sauce. Mix well. Top with fat-free cheese, if desired. Broil at 425 degrees for 3 minutes or until cheese is melted. Serve hot.

This can be made in advance, frozen and baked at 350 degrees for 35-45 minutes when needed.

♥ *Open-Faced Fresh Tomato Sandwiches* ♥

Kids Cookin'

Serves 4

0 Fat Grams

Prep Time:
10 minutes

Calories: 72

2   **pieces pocket bread, mini size**
    (I use Father Sam's)
8   **teaspoons fat-free ranch salad dressing**
    (I use Seven Seas)
1   **medium fresh tomato**
    (try to find the deepest red-colored one)

Cut pockets in half. Toast each half. Spread 2 teaspoons salad dressing on each half. Cut tomato into 4 slices. Put one slice tomato on each half of toasted pocket bread that has been spread with salad dressing. Eat immediately.

♥ *Asparagus Casserole Dinner* ♥

Serves 6

1.5 Fat Grams

Prep Time:
30 minutes

Calories: 256

8   redskin potatoes
1   pound fresh mushrooms, thinly sliced
½   pound turkey ham (or very lean ham),
     finely chopped
1   packet Butter Buds, dry
8   ounces fat-free cheddar cheese
     (I use Healthy Choice)
2   15-ounce cans long stem asparagus

Microwave the redskin potatoes until cooked. (It only takes a few minutes. Potatoes are tender when done.) While the potatoes are cooking, spray large skillet with a non-fat cooking spray. Sauté mushrooms, ham, and Butter Buds. Cut cooked redskins into ⅓-inch slices. Spray a 9 x 13-inch pan with a non-fat cooking spray. Arrange sliced cooked redskins in bottom of pan. Spread sautéed mushrooms and ham over potatoes. Arrange asparagus spears in strips. Sprinkle cheddar cheese on top, and broil for 3 to 5 minutes or until cheese is golden brown and hot.

How can we hope for greater gifts and talents from God if we don't even use the ones we have?

♥♥♥

♥ *Sauerkraut Spaghetti* ♥

Serves 1
2 Fat Grams
Prep Time: 15 minutes
Calories: 170

I know this recipe sounds crazy. To be honest, when I heard it from a friend I thought she was nuts, but my curiosity killed the cat! It's really good!

For however much you want to make, use this formula. This is for one serving.

½ **cup sauerkraut**
¾ **cup spaghetti sauce**
   (I use Prego Extra Chunky Garden Combination)
   Parmesan cheese (optional)

Drain sauerkraut and rinse. Squeeze dry. Mix spaghetti sauce with sauerkraut. Warm in the microwave. Sprinkle with grated Parmesan cheese, if desired. Serve warm.

Note: Calories can be cut 40 percent by using Healthy Choice Spaghetti Sauce.

♥ *Mexican Spaghetti* ♥

Serves 4
5.8 Grams Fat
Prep Time: 20 minutes
Calories: 260

For fast and easy Mexican Spaghetti Salad, do the exact same thing but serve chilled.

1 **cup shredded cooked beef**
2 **cups cooked spaghetti**
1 **16-ounce jar salsa**
   Fat-free taco or cheddar cheese, finely grated (optional)

Toss first three ingredients together. Top with cheese if desired. Microwave until warm. Serve warm. Serve extra warmed salsa on the side if desired.

Note: Leftover eye of round roast can be used.

♥ *Original Magic Pockets* ♥

(Fast & Easy)

These tasty delectables are fun for children to help make. Once I created one, it put me on a roll and I've created many different flavors. Don't limit yourself to just the ones I've created. Create some of your own!

♥ *Ham & Cheese Magic Pockets* ♥

Serves 15

1.4 Fat Grams

**Prep Time:
25 minutes**

Calories: 152

2   **egg whites**
3   **10-count cans Pillsbury Buttermilk Biscuits**
¾   **pound turkey ham, chopped into 1/4-inch pieces**
1   **cup fat-free cheddar cheese** (I use Healthy Choice)
½   **cup mushrooms, chopped** (optional)
2   **Tablespoons fat-free honey Dijon salad dressing**

Beat egg whites. Set aside. Spray two cookie sheets with a non-fat cooking spray. With hands, flatten each biscuit into a thin, flat piece of round dough. (That's where I have my children help out. While I'm chopping the ingredients, they flatten out the dough.) Arrange 15 individual flattened dough pieces on two cookie sheets making sure they do not touch. Lay extra dough pieces on wax paper until ready to use. Brush each dough piece with egg whites. (The beaten egg whites are the glue which holds the crust together and seals it shut.)

Preheat oven to 375 degrees. In a bowl, combine chopped ham, cheese, mushrooms, and honey dijon salad dressing. Mix until all ingredients are well coated with dressing. Put a rounded tablespoon of meat and cheese concoction in the center of each flattened dough piece on cookie sheet. Using remaining flattened dough, cover each one and brush sides with egg whites. Using a fork seal dough edges. Brush top with egg whites. Bake for 15 minutes.

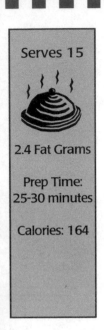

♥ *Pizza Magic Pockets* ♥

1   **pound ground eye of round** (beef)
2   **egg whites**
3   **10-count cans Pillsbury Buttermilk Biscuits**
1   **cup fat-free mozzarella finely shredded cheese** (I use Healthy Choice)
½   **cup mushrooms or green peppers** (Use any combination you desire)
½   **cup of your favorite pizza sauce** (I like Prego)
    Garlic salt (optional)

Brown beef and drain fat. Set aside. Beat egg whites. Set aside. Spray two cookie sheets with a non-fat cooking spray. With hands flatten each biscuit into a thin, flat piece of round dough. Arrange 15 individual flattened dough pieces on cookie sheets, making sure they do not touch. Brush each dough piece with beaten egg whites. Set aside.

Preheat oven to 375 degrees. In a bowl mix cheese, mushrooms, green peppers, browned meat, and pizza sauce together until well coated with sauce. Put a good size rounded tablespoon of meat and cheese concoction in the center of each flattened dough piece on cookie sheet. Using remaining flattened dough pieces, cover each one. Brush sides with egg whites. Using a fork, seal dough edges. Brush top with egg whites. Lightly sprinkle tops with garlic salt, if desired. Bake for 15 minutes.

♥ *South of the Border Magic Pockets* ♥

Serves 30

2.3 Fat Grams

Prep Time:
30 minutes

Calories: 171

2   **egg whites**
1   **pound ground eye of round** (beef)
1   **envelope taco seasoning for meat**
1   **cup corn**
2   **cups fat-free shredded cheddar cheese**
2   **Tablespoons sugar**
1   **cup chunky salsa**
6   **10-count cans of Pillsbury Buttermilk Biscuit dough**

Beat egg whites and set aside. Cook beef as directed on taco seasoning package; add taco seasoning. Mix all remaining ingredients — except for egg whites and dough — together until well blended. Spray four cookie sheets with a non-fat cooking spray.

Preheat oven 375 degrees. With hands, flatten 30 of the biscuits into round flat pieces and place on the cookie sheets. Make sure the edges do not touch each other. Brush each flattened dough piece with egg whites on the edges of the dough. Put one rounded tablespoon of meat concoction into center of each piece of flattened dough. With hands flatten one remaining biscuit for each pocket and cover each pocket, one at a time. Seal dough edges together with fork. Brush tops of each pocket with beaten egg whites. Sprinkle with paprika if desired. Bake for 15 minutes.

Serves 15

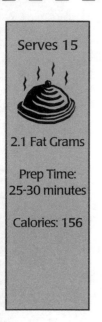

2.1 Fat Grams

Prep Time:
25-30 minutes

Calories: 156

♥ *Steak & Onion Philly Magic Pockets* ♥

2   **egg whites**
3   **10-count cans Pillsbury Buttermilk Biscuits**
½   **cup onion, finely chopped**
¾   **pound eye of round (beef), sliced into very thin strips, ¼ or ½-inch long**
¼   **cup steak sauce (I like Heinz 57)**
1   **cup fat-free shredded mozzarella cheese (I use Healthy Choice)**

Beat egg whites and set aside. Spray two cookie sheets with a non-fat cooking spray.

With hands, flatten each biscuit into a thin flat piece of round dough. Sauté onion with beef over low heat until thoroughly cooked (4 to 7 minutes). Remove from heat and let cool. Add steak sauce and cheese. Mix until well blended.

Preheat oven to 375 degrees. Arrange 15 pieces of flattened round dough pieces on cookie sheets so that sides do not touch. Brush sides with beaten egg whites. Put a good size tablespoon of meat and cheese concoction in the center of each flattened dough piece on cookie sheet. Using remaining flattened dough pieces, cover each one. With fork seal dough edges together. Brush top with egg whites. Bake for 15 minutes.

A happy heart is a thankful heart.

♥ *Complete Turkey &*
Dressing Dinner ♥

Serves 6

5 Fat Grams

Prep Time:
45 minutes

Calories: 225

This is so easy that it's almost embarrassing. But don't worry! This recipe can be made days in advance and refrigerated until ready to bake. Just cook a little longer to make sure it's completely warmed.

1   **box Stove Top stuffing, chicken or
    turkey flavor** (6-serving size)
2   **cups hot water**
2   **envelopes Butter Buds — dry**
12 **ounces turkey breast lunch meat**
    (I use Mr. Turkey)
1   **15-ounce can green beans, drained**
1   **12-ounce jar turkey gravy**
    (I use Heinz Homestyle)
    Pepper to taste (optional)

In medium bowl, mix seasoning from stuffing box with bread crumbs, water, and one envelope Butter Buds. Set aside. Preheat oven to 350 degrees. Spray a 9 x 13-inch pan with a non-fat cooking spray. Spread prepared stuffing mixture evenly on bottom of pan. Arrange turkey lunch meat slices on top of stuffing. (Edges of lunch meat should overlap.) Spread gravy evenly over turkey. Evenly arrange green beans on top of gravy. Sprinkle green beans with remaining envelope of Butter Buds and pepper, if desired. Cover pan with foil and bake covered for 30 to 35 minutes, until completely warmed.

Desserts

Desserts

♥ City Slicker S'more Balls ♥

Serves 15

.73 Fat Grams

Prep Time:
20 minutes

Calories: 55

Fun for kids to make! A neat indoor twist to S'mores that we make when we are camping.

2	**Tablespoons fat-free margarine** (I use Ultra Promise)
2	**cups mini marshmallows**
60	**chocolate chips**
3	**cups Golden Grahams Cereal**

Over low heat melt margarine and mix in mini marshmallows, stirring constantly.

When marshmallows have melted down to ½ of their original size, remove from heat. Add cereal and mix well. (Don't let marshmallows melt completely.)

Spray your hands with a non-fat cooking spray. Divide mixture into 15 parts. Roll each part with hands and form into balls. Place 4 chocolate chips throughout each ball.

Set each ball on wax paper and let cool completely.

♥ Chocolate Cherry Mousse ♥

♥

Serves 10

1 Fat Gram

Prep Time:
10 minutes

1	**large sugar-free chocolate pudding mix** (6 serving size)
1	**package Dream Whip — dry**
1½	**cups cold skim milk**
1	**15-ounce can lite cherry pie filling, chilled**

Mix together first 3 ingredients and blend until thick, about 3 minutes. Starting with and ending with cherry pie filling, alternate chocolate mousse and pie filling in a pretty glass (wine glasses, dessert cups, etc.). Keep chilled in refrigerator until ready to serve.

Refrigerate unused portions.

♥ Sweet & Heavenly Twinkie Dessert ♥

Serves 15

1.06 Fat Grams

Prep Time: 20-25 minutes

Calories: 138

2½   cups fresh strawberries, cleaned and cut into bite-sized pieces
1   cup sugar
3   Tablespoons cornstarch
2   Tablespoons Lite Karo Syrup
1   cup water
1   box sugar-free strawberry Jello, dry
9   Hostess Light Twinkies, cut in half lengthwise
¼   cup Cool Whip Free

In saucepan over medium low heat, mix sugar, cornstarch, syrup, and water. Bring to a boil. Stirring occasionally, cook until it becomes clear in color. Remove from heat. Let cool a couple of minutes. In the meantime, line a 9 x 13-inch pan with the cut Twinkies, cream side up. Edges will be touching. Stir strawberry sugar-free Jello into clear mixture. Mix well until it is one smooth color of red. Add strawberries. Spread strawberries over Twinkies. Refrigerate for 5 minutes before serving. Top with a dab of Cool Whip and cut it into the top of the dessert with knife to make it look pretty.

Refrigerate unused portions.

♥ *Cherry Berry Dessert Waffles* ♥

Serves 1

0 Fat Grams

Prep Time:
20 minutes

Calories: 248

This is a beautiful dessert to the eyes and a special dessert for any occasion. This is so filling that I eat it as a meal.

1   **Special K fat-free waffle**
3   **ounces sugar-free, fat-free blueberry ribbon frozen dessert**
     (I use Superior Dairy)
1/2 **cup lite cherry pie filling**
     (Meijer has a good, inexpensive brand)
1   **Tablespoon Cool Whip Free**
1   **Tablespoon lite blueberry syrup**
     (I use Featherweight)

Pop waffle into the toaster until golden brown. While still warm, put blueberry ribbon dessert on waffle. Top with cherry pie filling and add a dab of Cool Whip on top. Drizzle lite blueberry syrup over dessert, and serve immediately.

Refrigerate unused portions.

♥ *Chocolate Mousse* ♥

♥

Serves 6

0 Fat Grams

Prep Time:
10 minutes

Calories: 78

1   **box sugar-free instant chocolate pudding mix (4 serving size)**
3   **Tablespoons fat-free hot fudge syrup**
     (I use Smucker's)
1   **8-ounce carton Cool Whip Free**

Mix all together until smooth. Serve chilled.

Refrigerate unused portions.

♥ *Whitney Crispies* ♥

An excellent twist to an old favorite! (Created by my six-year-old daughter, Whitney.)

¼ **cup fat-free margarine**
   (I use Ultra Promise)
1 **10-ounce package mini marshmallows +**
   1 cup mini marshmallows
1 **teaspoon peanut butter flavor extract**
5 **cups toasted rice cereal**
⅓ **cup fat-free chocolate frosting (recipe in**
   book, or use Lovin' Lites Chocolate Frosting)

Spray Dutch Oven or large saucepan with a non-fat cooking spray. Melt together margarine, marshmallows and peanut butter extract. Remove from heat. Stir in cereal. Press into a 9 x 13-inch pan that has been sprayed with a non-fat cooking spray. Let cool. Frost with chocolate frosting.

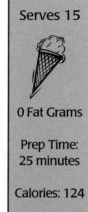

Serves 15

0 Fat Grams

Prep Time:
25 minutes

Calories: 124

♥ *Warm Fruit Cocktail Dessert* ♥

Great for cold, snowy days.

1 **16-ounce can lite fruit cocktail with its**
   juice
1 **9-ounce Jiffy Golden Yellow Cake mix**
   — dry
   Cool Whip Free

Preheat oven to 350 degrees. Drain juice from fruit cocktail, retaining juice. Beat cake mix and fruit cocktail juice together until well blended. Gently mix fruit with spoon into cake batter until well blended. Spray 8 x 8-inch or a 9 x 9-inch square cake pan with a non-fat cooking spray. Pour cake batter into prepared pan. Bake for 40-45 minutes or until top is golden brown. Serve warm with Cool Whip Free. You need to spoon out this dessert; it will not cut.

Refrigerate unused portions.

♥
Serves 9

2 Grams Fat

Prep Time:
60 minutes

Calories: 133
(not including
Cool Whip)

♥ *Warm Baked Peach Dessert* ♥

Serves 6

.1 Fat Grams

Prep Time:
25 minutes

Calories: 169

1   **29-ounce can peaches in lite syrup or own juices**
1   **7-ounce box Health Valley Fat-free Peach Apricot Mini Fruit Center Cookies**
¼   **cup Mrs. Richardson's Butterscotch Caramel Fudge Topping**

Preheat oven to 350 degrees. Pour peaches with juices in an 8 x 10-inch pan. Crumble cookies on top. Microwave caramel fudge on high for 10 to 15 seconds (just enough to drizzle). Drizzle caramel over cookie crumbs. Bake for 20 minutes. Serve hot from the oven.

Great with fat-free frozen vanilla yogurt.

Refrigerate unused portions.

♥ *Blueberry Drops* ♥

♥

Yields 90

.009 Fat
Grams

Prep Time:
20 minutes

Calories: 42

2   **cups blueberry pie filling** (21-ounce can minus 2 Tablespoons)
2   **16-ounce boxes angel food cake mixes** (I use Pillsbury)

Preheat oven to 350 degrees. In a large bowl, mix pie filling with cake mixes by slowly adding 1 cup of the cake mix at a time to the filling. Spray a cookie sheet with non-fat cooking spray and drop batter by the teaspoon onto cookie sheet. Bake for 8 to 10 minutes — until bottoms are golden brown. Once cooled, the golden brown bottoms will be crispy.

♥ *Cinnamon Krispie Squares* ♥

If you like Rice Krispie Squares and cinnamon, you'll love these.

- 1   **10.5-ounce bag mini marshmallows**
- 8   **cups Apple Cinnamon Rice Krispies**
       (Kellogg's)
- 3   **Tablespoons fat-free margarine**
       (I use Ultra Promise)
- 2   **teaspoons cinnamon**
- 1   **teaspoon NutraSweet Spoonful** (OR
       1 teaspoon sugar)

Spray a 9 x 13-inch pan with non-fat cooking spray. Set aside. Mix 1 teaspoon cinnamon and 1 teaspoon NutraSweet together. Set aside. In large Dutch Oven or saucepan, melt margarine and marshmallows together over low heat, with remaining 1 teaspoon cinnamon, stirring constantly. Once marshmallows are melted, remove from heat. Stir in the Apple Cinnamon Rice Krispies. Mix until well coated with marshmallow mixture. Press into prepared 9 x 13-inch pan. Sprinkle top with prepared cinnamon/NutraSweet topping. Refrigerate for 15 minutes. Cut into squares.

Yields 30

0 Fat Grams

Prep Time:
25-30 minutes

With
NutraSweet—
Calories: 76
With sugar —
Calories: 77

The prettiest thing you can wear is a smile.

♥ *Fat-free Granola Bars* ♥

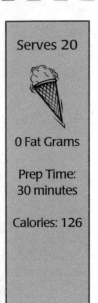

Serves 20

0 Fat Grams

Prep Time:
30 minutes

Calories: 126

This homemade version will save you bundles of money!

1	**10.5-ounce bag of mini marshmallows**
¼	**cup fat-free margarine** **(I use Ultra Promise)**
3½	**cups fat-free granola** **(I use Health Valley, 12-ounce size)**
½	**cup raisins**
2	**cups Rice Krispies**

In a large Dutch Oven pan melt margarine and marshmallows over low heat, stirring constantly. Once marshmallows are melted, remove from heat. Add granola, raisins and Rice Krispies. Mix well.

Spray a cookie sheet with edges (approximately 15 x 10-inch with ½-inch edge) with a non-fat cooking spray. Pour onto sheet. Spray palm of hand with non-fat spray. With palm of hand press granola mixture firmly down. Let cool.

Cut into 20 bars. Wrap individual bars with plastic wrap. Keep in a cool, dry place.

For tropical fat-free granola bars: Substitute ¼ cup chopped dried pineapple and ¼ cup chopped dried papaya for the raisins.

Cranberry granola bars: Substitute ½ cup dried cranberries.

♥ *Butterscotch Cake Sundaes* ♥

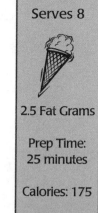
1   **4-serving size fat-free butterscotch
    pudding mix** (OR you could substitute an
    already prepared fat-free pudding, in the dairy
    section)
2   **cups skim milk**
1   **12-ounce angel food cake** (OR use 12
    ounces of larger cake)
1   **ounce finely chopped pecans**
8   **teaspoons fat-free hot fudge, warmed**

Prepare pudding as directed on box, using skim milk. After
pudding has thickened, tear the angel food cake up into
bite-sized pieces and put into the pudding. Add half of the
finely chopped pecans to pudding. Mix pudding, cake, and
pecans by hand until cake pieces are well-coated. Spoon equally
into 8 individual dessert cups or into a large serving bowl.
Microwave hot fudge until easy to drizzle. Drizzle hot fudge over
dessert and sprinkle remaining pecans. Keep refrigerated until
ready to serve. Serve chilled.

♥ *Chocolate Cheesecake* ♥

Serves 20

2.5 Fat Grams

Prep Time:
20 minutes

With Equal —
Calories: 125
With sugar —
Calories: 137

½   **cup fat-free margarine, melted**
     (I use Ultra Promise)
2   **packets Equal** (OR 1 Tablespoon and 1 teaspoon
     sugar)
     Graham cracker crumbs from mix
2   **9-ounce packages lite Royal cheesecake**
1   **package sugar-free instant chocolate**
     pudding
2   **Tablespoons cocoa** (baking cocoa)
6   **packets of Equal** (OR 1/4 cup sugar)
3   **cups skim milk**
⅓   **jar fat-free hot fudge**
     (I use Smucker's)

Mix margarine, 2 packets Equal and graham cracker crumbs
together well. Spray a 9 x 13-inch pan with non-fat cooking spray
and press crust into pan with fork.

In a large bowl, beat remaining ingredients for 3 minutes on low
speed. Pour cream mixture over crust. Melt hot fudge in
microwave. With spoon drizzle hot fudge over chocolate
cheesecake. Refrigerate. Serve chilled.

Refrigerate unused portions.

Those who are
thankful for
the little
things in life
are the ones
who enjoy life
to the fullest.

♥♥♥

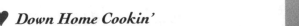

Kids Cookin'

♥ *Flower Pot Pudding* ♥

Set a gummy worm next to flowers for fun if you'd like.

Serves 4

2.8 Fat Grams

Prep Time:
25 minutes

Calories: 132

8	reduced fat SnackWell's chocolate cream filled cookies, with cream removed
1	4-serving size box sugar-free chocolate pudding
2	cups skim milk
4	small flower pots or foam coffee cups
4	small bouquets of silk flowers
4	Gummy worms (optional)

Crush cookies, set aside. Prepare pudding as directed on box, using skim milk. Put ⅛ of cookie crumbs in bottom of each flower pot or coffee cup. Put ¼ of pudding in each cup. Top each with remaining cookie crumbs. Stick small bouquet in each pot. Chill. Serve chilled.

Refrigerate unused portions.

♥ *Cherry Pineapple Cake* ♥

So good! So delicious! So easy!

Serves 15

2 Fat Grams

Prep Time: 35 minutes

Calories: 163

1   **box Betty Crocker Super Moist yellow cake mix with pudding in the mix**
1   **21-ounce can "lite" cherry pie filling**
1   **20-ounce can crushed pineapple, drained**

Preheat oven to 350 degrees. Mix above ingredients all together. Spray a 9 x 13-inch cake pan with a non-fat cooking spray and flour. Pour batter in pan and bake for 30 to 35 minutes or until knife inserted in center comes out clean.

This is excellent served warm with Dream Whip or no-fat frozen yogurt.

Refrigerate unused portions.

♥ *Blueberry Cake* ♥

♥

Serves 20

.008 Fat Grams

Prep Time: 30 minutes

Calories: 102 (cake only)

1   **cup blueberry pie filling**
1   **16-ounce box angel food cake mix (I use Pillsbury) — dry**

Preheat oven to 350 degrees. Mix pie filling and angel food cake mix together. Spray 9 x 13-inch pan with non-fat cooking spray and pour batter into pan. Bake for 25 to 28 minutes, or until top is deep golden brown and cracks appear on the top. Cool completely. Serve with a little dab of remaining pie filling if desired.

Also great as a snack-cake-type finger food.

Refrigerate unused portions.

♥ *Tootie-Fruity Coffee Cake* ♥

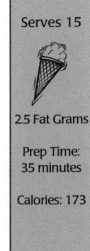

Serves 15

2.5 Fat Grams

Prep Time:
35 minutes

Calories: 173

Use as a coffee cake for breakfast or use as a snack cake.

- 2 **egg whites**
- 1 **16-ounce can "lite" fruit cocktail**
- 1 **box Betty Crocker Super Moist yellow cake mix with pudding in the mix**
- 1 **envelope Dream Whip, dry**
- 2 **Tablespoons powdered sugar**
- 1 **teaspoon cinnamon**
- ⅓ **cup flour**

Preheat oven to 350 degrees. Beat eggs until bubbly. Add fruit cocktail with its juices and cake mix. Beat at low speed until well blended. Spray a 9 x 13-inch pan with a non-fat cooking spray. Spread batter in pan. Mix remaining ingredients by hand until well blended. Sprinkle on top of cake. Bake cake with topping for 30 minutes, or until knife inserted in middle comes out clean.

Refrigerate unused portions.

♥ *Whatcha' Macallit Sundae* ♥

Serves 1

1.5 Fat Grams

Prep Time:
15 minutes

Calories: 385

This is so rich you may want to share.

1 **1.1-ounce fat-free brownie**
½ **cup fat-free chocolate frozen yogurt**
1 **Tablespoon Hershey Fat-free Syrup**
1 **Tablespoon Mrs. Richardson's Fat-free**
   Butterscotch Caramel Fudge Syrup
11 **chocolate chips**
3 **SnackWell's Mini Chocolate Chip cookies,**
   broken into pieces

Top the fat-free brownie with fat-free chocolate frozen yogurt, Hershey's syrup, butterscotch caramel fudge, chocolate chips, and top with cookie pieces. Serve immediately.

Triple this recipe, add pickle spears and serve at 3:00 a.m. It'll satisfy any pregnant lady's late night cravings!

Hang around
quality people.

♥♥♥

♥ *Apple Cinnamon Cake* ♥

Serves 15

2 Fat Grams

Prep Time:
40 minutes

Calories: 169

1   **box yellow lite cake mix**
      (I use Betty Crocker Super Moist)
1½ **cups unsweetened applesauce**
2   **teaspoons cinnamon**

Preheat oven to 350 degrees. Mix all ingredients in blender on medium speed until completely mixed (approximately 1½ to 2 minutes). Spray a 9 x 13-inch cake pan with a non-fat cooking spray and pour batter into pan. Bake for 35 minutes.

Glaze frosting:
  ½ **cup brown sugar (either lite or dark)**
  ½ **cup powdered sugar**
  5 **Tablespoons applesauce**
  ½ **teaspoon cinnamon**

Mix all ingredients in blender on medium speed until completely mixed (approximately 1½ to 2 minutes). Once cake is removed from oven, immediately spread glaze frosting over top of cake while the cake is still warm. Let cake cool completely before covering. Refrigerate cake. Good served either chilled or at room temperature.

Refrigerate unused portions.

Serves 12

3.6 Fat Grams

Prep Time:
25-30 minutes
(freeze 2
hours)

Calories: 184

♥ *Frozen Chocolate Cherry Cordial Cake* ♥

Our family loves the frozen yogurt cakes that can be bought at specialty stores, but with the high cost of them I learned to make my own. They're fast to create. A huge hit every time!

6   **fudge cream wafers**
    (I use Dutch Twin Reduced — 5 Fat Grams — 130 calories)
99 **chocolate chips**
13 **maraschino cherries**
½   **gallon fat-free frozen chocolate yogurt, softened**

Topping:
33 **chocolate chips**
1   **Tablespoon Hershey's Chocolate Syrup**
5   **maraschino cherries, cut in half** (optional)

Grind wafers in blender for a few seconds, until finely crumbled. Spray an 8-inch cheesecake pan (where sides of pan can be released if desired) with a non-fat cooking spray. Evenly sprinkle wafer crumbs on bottom of pan. Do not press crumbs! Chop 99 chocolate chips and 13 cherries in food processor or blender.

In a large bowl, stir chocolate chips and cherries into frozen yogurt until well mixed. Spread frozen yogurt mixture evenly over wafer crumbs. Arrange remaining 33 chocolate chips and maraschino cherries on top of cake. Drizzle with 1 Tablespoon chocolate syrup. Freeze for 2 hours. (Takes 1 hour to set.) Keep in freezer until ready to use.

♥ *Banana Split Cake* ♥

Serves 15

4.53 Fat
Grams

Prep Time:
45 minutes

With
NutraSweet—
Calories: 236
With sugar —
Calories: 242

1   20-ounce can crushed pineapple in its
own juice, no sugar added

1   18.25-ounce box "lite" yellow cake mix
(I use Betty Crocker Super Moist) — dry

Preheat oven to 350 degrees. Mix pineapple juice with cake
on medium speed for 2 to 3 minutes until well blended.
Spray a 9 x 13-inch pan with a non-fat cooking spray and
pour batter into pan. Bake for 40 minutes, or until
toothpick put into the center of cake comes out clean. Let
cool. Once cake is completely cooled, add topping to cake.

Topping:

2   Tablespoons NutraSweet Spoonful (OR 2
Tablespoon sugar)

1   can "lite" cherry pie filling

2   bananas, thinly sliced

1   8-ounce carton Cool Whip Free

2   Tablespoons Hershey's Chocolate Syrup

In bowl, mix NutraSweet well into pie filling. Spread cherry pie
filling over completely cooled cake. Press banana slices lightly into
pie filling. Spread Cool Whip over bananas. With spoon drizzle
chocolate syrup over Cool Whip. Keep chilled until ready to serve.
Refrigerate unused portions.

♥ *Chocolate Cherry Chunk Frozen Cake* ♥

This dessert which appears to be painstakingly long to prepare is super easy, and just as delicious! This is totally excellent!

3   **chocolate sandwich cookies**
      (I use Healthy Choice)
3   **Tablespoons water**
1   **package fudge brownie mix, smart size**
      (I use Gold Medal) — **dry**
9   **maraschino cherries, cut in half**
2   **quarts cherry chocolate flake low-fat frozen yogurt, slightly thawed**
      (I use Flavorite)

Remove cream center from cookies and discard. Crush cookies fine. (I use a blender.) Set aside. With fork, stir water into brownie mix until mixture is coarse and crumbly. Spray 8-inch cheese cake pan with non-fat cooking spray. Press ½ of the brownie mixture onto bottom of pan. DO NOT BAKE!!

Gently spoon slightly thawed frozen yogurt over brownie crust. With knife, smooth the top of the yogurt. Add cookie crumbs to remaining brownie crumbs. Stir until well mixed. Put on top of yogurt. Top will still look crumbly. Arrange cherry halves on top of crumbs. Freeze for 2 hours.

♥ *S'more Ice Cream Cake* ♥

Takes time to freeze.

1½	**cups graham cracker crumbs**
5	**packets Equal** (OR 1/4 cup sugar)
4	**Tablespoons water**
2	**quarts fat-free chocolate ice cream, softened** (I use Meadow Gold)
1⅔	**cups mini marshmallows**
¼	**cup semi-sweet chocolate chips**

Mix graham cracker crumbs, Equal, and water together until mixture is moist, yet crumbly. In large bowl stir together ice cream, marshmallows, and chocolate chips until well blended. Spray an 8-inch cheesecake pan, with sides that release, with a non-fat cooking spray. Press ½ of the graham cracker crumb mixture onto bottom of pan. Pour ice cream mixture over crust. Evenly sprinkle remaining graham cracker crumb mixture on top of ice cream mixture. Freeze for 2 hours or overnight.

Serves 12

3.2 Fat Grams

Prep Time:
20 minutes
(Freeze 2 hours)

With Equal —
Calories: 207
With sugar —
Calories: 222

♥ *Marshmallow Applesauce Dessert* ♥

4	**cups applesauce**
¼	**teaspoon allspice**
½	**teaspoon cinnamon**
2	**cups mini marshmallows** (OR quartered regular marshmallows)

Preheat oven to 350 degrees. Mix applesauce and seasonings together. Pour into a 9 x 13-inch pan. Sprinkle with marshmallows. Bake for 10 minutes. Serve warm.

Refrigerate unused portions.

♥

Serves 15

.1 Fat Grams

Prep Time:
20 minutes

Calories: 71

♥ *Brownie Dough Frozen Cake* ♥

Serves 12

5.6 Fat Grams

Prep Time:
25 minutes
(Freeze 2
hours)

Calories: 177

I got this idea from cookie dough ice cream. If you like brownies and cookie dough, you'll love this creation. It's one of my favorites. Beware! It's rich and filling even though low in fat.

3   **Tablespoons water**
1   **10-serving size package fudge brownie**
    mix* (I use Gold Medal, smart size)
3   **Tablespoons fat-free hot fudge**
    (I use Smucker's)
2   **quarts Swiss chocolate almond low-fat**
    frozen yogurt, softened
    (I use Flavorite)

Mix water with brownie mix. Spray 8-inch cheesecake pan, with sides that can be released,** with non-fat cooking spray. Press ⅔ brownie mix into bottom of pan, using a fork sprayed with non-fat cooking spray. DO NOT BAKE! Set aside.

In large bowl, use fingers to slowly work marble-size pieces of the remaining brownie dough into frozen yogurt. Smooth frozen yogurt/brownie mixture into pan over brownie dough. Microwave hot fudge and drizzle over cake. Freeze for 2 hours or until set.

Dip knife into hot water. Run knife along edge of pan. Take sides off of pan. Cut into 12 wedges.

*If you want to use a large size brand, portion out 10 serving size and bake the rest for brownies.

**If you don't have a cheesecake pan, a regular cake pan will work fine.

♥ *Cranberry Cake* ♥

Great served warm with a dab of Cool Whip Free or chilled as a snack cake.

1   **box super moist yellow cake mix** (I use **Betty Crocker with pudding in the mix**) — **dry**

1   **16-ounce can jellied cranberry sauce** (I use Ocean Spray)

Preheat oven to 350 degrees. Spray 9 x 13-inch pan with non-fat cooking spray. Set aside. Set aside 1/2 cup of the boxed cake mix. With mixer, blend together cranberry sauce and remaining cake mix on low speed. Once well mixed, increase speed to high. Beat on high for 2 minutes. Spread smoothly into prepared pan. Sprinkle with remaining dry cake mix on top. Bake for 30 to 32 minutes or until top is golden brown.

Refrigerate unused portions.

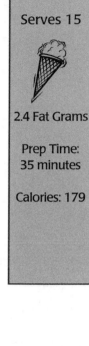

Serves 15

2.4 Fat Grams

Prep Time: 35 minutes

Calories: 179

♥ *Creamy Fat-Free Chocolate Frosting* ♥

¾   **cup fat-free margarine** (I use **Ultra Promise**)

¾   **cup cocoa**

1   **teaspoon vanilla**

4-5   **packets Equal** (OR 3 Tablespoons more powdered sugar)

3½-4   **cups powdered sugar**

Mix margarine, cocoa, vanilla and Equal together with mixer on low speed until well-blended. Slowly add powdered sugar. Beat until creamy smooth.

♥

Serves 24

.4 Fat Grams

Prep Time: 8 minutes

With Equal — Calories: 87
With sugar — Calories: 91

♥ *Pistachio-Nut Snack Cake* ♥

1   **cup applesauce**
8   **egg whites**
1   **cup water**
2   **4-serving size boxes sugar-free pistachio pudding**
1   **box yellow cake mix**
      (I use Betty Crocker Super Moist with pudding in the mix)

Preheat oven to 350 degrees. Beat applesauce, egg whites, and water with mixer on high for 30 seconds. Add pudding and cake mix. Beat on medium speed for 2 minutes. Spray three 8-inch cake pans with a non-fat cooking spray. Pour batter evenly into pans. Bake for 30 minutes.

If desired, frost with prepared Dream Whip or eat without topping as a snack cake.

Refrigerate unused portions.

♥ *Brownie Melt-A-Ways* ♥

Brownie is the nickname of our youngest child. I named these after her. The marshmallows were her idea.

1   **21.5-ounces box fudge brownie mix**
      (I use Betty Crocker)
3   **egg whites**
3   **Tablespoons water**
5   **ounces mini marshmallows**

Preheat oven to 350 degrees. Mix brownie mix, egg whites, and water. Spray jelly roll pan with non-fat spray. Spread mixture thinly on pan. Press marshmallows onto mixture. Bake for 15 minutes. The tips of marshmallows will be toasty brown. Cool and cut into 48 little squares. Store in refrigerator.

Section 2

Recipes That Take More Time or Preparation

Appetizers
Snacks
Beverages

Appetizers, Snacks, Beverages

♥ *"Yum to Your Tum"*
Appetizers ♥

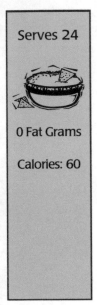

Serves 24

0 Fat Grams

Calories: 60

8 **ounces fat-free cream cheese**
   (I use Healthy Choice)
3 **Tablespoons chunky salsa**
1 **Tablespoon + 1 teaspoon reduced calorie
   ranch dressing mix**
   (I use Hidden Valley)
10 **fat-free flour tortillas**
   (I like Buena Vista)
4 **cups finely chopped lettuce**
1 **cup salsa for dipping** (if desired)
1 **teaspoon Tabasco sauce** (optional)

Note: You will use 5 flour tortillas for each stack. Then you will cut each stack into 12 pieces of pie.

In medium bowl, mix first three ingredients until well blended. Spread about 2½ Tablespoons of cream mixture on tortilla. Top with ½ cup finely chopped lettuce. Repeat this process three more times. Top with fifth tortilla. With hands press top firmly down. Cut into 12 pie wedges. If desired, when eating use salsa for dipping.

If you like a spicier appetizer, add 1 teaspoon Tabasco sauce to cream mixture.

♥ *Stuffed Mushrooms* ♥

Serves 7

1.6 Fat Grams

Calories: 74

1	cup turkey ham, finely chopped
½	cup onion, finely chopped
1	Tablespoon fat-free margarine (I use Ultra Promise)
1	teaspoon garlic powder Pinch of ground sage
½	cup Italian style bread crumbs
1	Tablespoon grated Parmesan cheese
12-14	large fresh mushrooms, cleaned, with stems taken out Molly McButter Sour Cream flavored powdered substitute

Preheat oven to 350 degrees. Spray skillet with non-fat cooking spray. Brown onions and ham for a couple of minutes. Add fat-free margarine, garlic, and sage. Stir until well blended. Remove from heat. Add bread crumbs and Parmesan cheese. With fingers stuff each prepared mushroom cup. Sprinkle with sour cream flavored substitute. Bake for 20 minutes. Serve warm.

♥ *Ham & Onion Roll-ups* ♥

♥

Serving Size
2 pieces
(not cut)

1 Fat Gram

With Equal —
Calories: 48
With sugar —
Calories: 52

¾	cup non-fat cottage cheese
1	package reduced calorie ranch salad dressing mix (I use Hidden Valley)
1	packet Equal (OR 2 teaspoons sugar)
4	ounces fat-free cream cheese
¾	cup non-fat sour cream
3	Tablespoon water
1	slice very thin ham (I use Oscar Mayer Deli Thin)
1	fresh green onion

With mixer on high, beat cottage cheese for 1 to 2 minutes until smooth and creamy. Add everything but ham and onion. Beat on medium until well blended. Spread a thin layer of vegetable dip on ham. Starting from the smallest part of ham slice, roll the green onion up with the ham. If you'd like, you can slice the long ham/onion roll-up into thirds or halves and place on fat-free crackers.

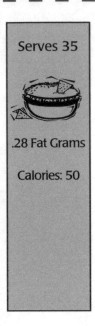

Serves 35

.28 Fat Grams

Calories: 50

♥ *Vegetable Pizza* ♥

2	**10-count cans Pillsbury Buttermilk Biscuits (20 biscuits total)**
½	**cup fat-free sour cream**
½	**cup fat-free mayonnaise**
8	**ounces fat-free cream cheese, softened**
1	**1.1-ounce packet reduced calorie ranch dressing mix (I use Hidden Valley)**
	Chopped fresh vegetables

Preheat oven to 425 degrees. Knead all biscuit dough together and roll out on floured surface. Spray a cookie sheet, with edges (15 x 9 ¼-inch), with a non-fat cooking spray. Press dough out onto cookie sheet, covering whole sheet. With fork poke holes all over through the dough. Bake for 7 to 9 minutes, until golden brown.

In large bowl, beat remaining ingredients with mixer at medium speed until well mixed. Spread mixture onto crust, covering all the way to the sides. Cover with your favorite fresh, chopped vegetables. I like red peppers, green peppers, mushrooms, broccoli, carrots, cherry tomatoes, and celery.

♥ *Spinach Balls (The Healthy Ones!)* ♥

Serves 12

1.6 Fat Grams

Calories: 89

Great as an appetizer or a side dish with pork.

- 2   **packages frozen chopped spinach, drained**
- 1   **package stuffing mix with seasoning — dry**
- 1½ **cups Egg Beaters** (OR 12 egg whites)
- 1   **teaspoon garlic powder**
- ¾   **cup melted Butter Buds** (OR fat-free margarine)
- 1   **onion, chopped**
- ¼   **cup Parmesan cheese**

Preheat oven to 350 degrees. Mix thawed spinach and stuffing. Set aside. In a bowl, combine the remaining ingredients, then mix into spinach mixture. Chill. Form into balls. Spray cookie sheet with non-fat cookie spray and arrange balls so that they do not touch. Bake for 20 minutes.

Kids Cookin'

♥ *Julie Casillas's Mexican Dip* ♥

Serves 12

0 Fat Grams

Prep Time: minutes

Calories: 39 (without chips)

- 1   **can Health Valley fat-free chili with beans**
         (I find this at Kroger's)
- 2   **8-ounce packages fat-free cream cheese**
         Salsa (optional)
         Chopped onion (optional)

Mix together, put in Crock-Pot, heat and serve. Serve with your favorite brand of low-fat tortilla chips.

Breads

&

Rolls

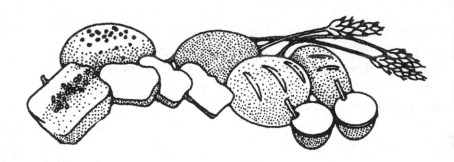

Breads & Rolls

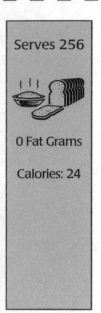
♥ *My Grandma Schaefer's Apple Butter* ♥

This is absolutely, positively the best and easiest apple butter I have ever eaten! You haven't had apple butter till you've had this!

10 **cups cooked apples** (about 12 large apples, cored) **cooked in about ¼ cup water**
6   **cups sugar**
1   **teaspoon cinnamon**
1   **teaspoon allspice**
½   **teaspoon ground cloves**

Put cooked apples in blender. Beat until all is ground up. Add remaining ingredients and cook in Crock-Pot for 17 hours. Stir once in awhile. Take lid off for last two hours. Fill canning jar ½-inch shy of the top. Melt paraffin and pour over.

If you don't want to can it, just keep it refrigerated. Our family eats it up fast! I love to eat this with fat-free cottage cheese.

Be a blessing to others.

♥♥♥

♥ *Mmm! Ma! Ma! Mia' Bread!* ♥

Great with Italian food. Makes 2 jelly roll pans.

1	package yeast
1½	cups warm water
1	teaspoon salt
1	Tablespoon sugar
2	cups whole wheat flour
2	cups self-rising flour
½	cup liquid Butter Buds (¼ cup per pan)
2	teaspoons garlic salt (1 teaspoon per pan)
2	teaspoons basil (1 teaspoon per pan)
2	teaspoons oregano (1 teaspoon per pan)
½	cup grated Parmesan cheese (¼ cup per pan)

Preheat oven to 425 degrees. Dissolve yeast in warm water.
Add salt and sugar, stir until dissolved in the water. Add both
kinds of flour to water mixture. Knead on lightly floured surface.
Spray two jelly roll pans with non-fat spray. Divide the dough in
half and place in pans. Roll out dough to edges of pan with rolling
pin. Spread ¼ cup of liquid Butter Buds onto each pan of dough.
Sprinkle with garlic salt, basil, oregano, and Parmesan cheese. Bake
for 15 to 20 minutes or until crust is nice and brown. Serve warm.

Serves 36

.4 Fat Grams

Calories: 94

♥ *Yummy Whole Wheat Pretzels* ♥

These are fun to make with your children! Rather than just making pretzel shapes only, our children and I like to make unique and fun shapes such as hearts, balloons, a kiss, etc. Be creative and have fun!

2	**packages yeast**
3	**cups warm water**
2	**teaspoon salt** (coarse salt, if desired)
2	**Tablespoons sugar**
5	**cups whole wheat flour**
3	**cups self-rising flour**
2	**egg whites, beaten**

Preheat oven to 425 degrees. Dissolve yeast in warm water. Add salt and sugar to water and stir until dissolved. Add both kinds of flour and stir until combined. Knead on lightly floured surface. Separate into 36 individual balls. Roll each ball between hands until dough is long enough to make into a large pretzel (12 to 15 inches). Spray a cookie sheet with non-fat spray and place pretzels on sheet. Brush with beaten egg whites. If desired, sprinkle lightly with coarse salt. Bake for 10 to 12 minutes or until the tips of pretzels are slightly brown.

♥ *Cinnamon Oatmeal Muffins* ♥

1	box yellow cake mix (I prefer Betty Crocker Super Moist with pudding in the mix) — dry
2	Tablespoons cinnamon
½	cup oatmeal
1½	cups water
4	egg whites

Preheat oven to 350 degrees. Mix all ingredients together until well blended. Spray muffin tins with a non-fat cooking spray, and pour batter evenly into cups.

Crumb topping:

1	Tablespoon cinnamon
3	Tablespoons whole wheat flour
4	Tablespoons oatmeal
½	cup dark brown sugar
2	Tablespoons fat-free margarine (I use Ultra Promise Fat-free)

With fork mix until dry and crumbly. With fingers sprinkle on top of muffin batter already in tins. Bake 25 minutes.

Serves 12

2.9 Fat Grams

Calories: 188

♥ *Very Berry Muffins* ♥

1	cup your favorite berries
1½	cups whole wheat flour
2	cups all purpose flour
1½	Tablespoons NutraSweet Spoonful (or 1½ Tablespoons sugar)
5	teaspoons baking powder
2	teaspoons lite salt
1½	cups water
⅔	cup applesauce
4	egg whites, beaten just until foamy
4	Tablespoons sugar
	Your favorite berry preserves

Preheat oven to 400 degrees. Combine all ingredients, except berries, and stir by hand just until moistened. Batter will be lumpy. Carefully fold berries into batter. Spray muffin tins with a non-fat cooking spray. Fill cups ⅔ full. Put 2 teaspoons preserves on top of batter in each muffin cup before baking. Bake for 20 minutes (longer for larger muffins).

♥

Serves 12

.5 Fat Grams

With NutraSweet — Calories: 163
With sugar — Calories: 169

Serving size:
1 muffin

Calories
(approximate):
Mini – 50
Large – 200

1	cup liquid Butter Buds
2	cups brown sugar
⅓	cup Sugar Twin brown sugar replacement
8	egg whites
1	teaspoon cinnamon
1	teaspoon nutmeg
1	teaspoon lite salt
1	cup canned pumpkin
⅔	cup water
2	cups whole wheat flour
1	cup flour
2	teaspoons baking soda

Preheat oven to 350 degrees. Mix first eight ingredients until smooth. Add water, flours, and baking soda. Spray muffin tins with a non-fat cooking spray. Using NutraSweet coat insides of muffin tins as you would with flour. Fill tins up to rim with batter.

Crumb topping:

1	Tablespoon dry Butter Buds
1	Tablespoon sugar
1	teaspoon brown sugar
1	teaspoon flour
1	teaspoon cinnamon
4	teaspoons water

With fork, mix all ingredients listed above until mixture is crumbly. Sprinkle topping on muffins before baking. Lightly sprinkle NutraSweet on top of crumb topping. Bake mini muffins 30 to 35 minutes and large muffins 40 to 45 minutes, or until knife inserted in center comes out clean. Good served warm.

Like yourself,
God does.

♥ *Bran Banana Muffins* ♥

Serves 12

.7 Fat Grams

Calories: 104

1¾   cups whole wheat flour
2   teaspoons baking powder
½   teaspoon ground cloves
½   teaspoon lite salt
¼   cup oat bran
½   cup bran cereal (I use Nabisco 100% Bran)
4   egg whites
⅓   cup water
1   package Butter Buds, dry
4   medium ripe bananas, mashed

Preheat oven to 350 degrees. Soak bran cereal in water until soft. Add egg whites and mix until well blended. Add remaining ingredients and mix until all is blended. Spray muffin pans with a non-fat cooking spray and pour batter evenly into cups.

Topping:
⅓   cup flour
⅓   cup sugar
1   package Butter Buds, dry
1   teaspoon vanilla
1-2   teaspoons water (just enough to make topping crumbly)

Mix topping with fork until coarse and crumbly. Sprinkle on top of batter. Baking time depends on muffin tin size:

Mini — approximately 15 minutes

Regular — approximately 25 to 30 minutes

Large — approximately 35 to 40 minutes

Bake until knife inserted in middle comes out clean.

Soups
Salads
Vegetables

Soups, Salads, Vegetables

Serves 21

1.8 Fat Grams

Calories: 114

♥ *Beef Barley Soup* ♥

1	pound ground eye of round (beef)
2	medium onions, diced
4	medium tomatoes, diced
2	Tablespoons garlic salt
1	Tablespoon fresh basil
12	cups water
1	16-ounce bag of frozen mixed vegetables
	(carrots, peas, corn, green beans and lima beans)
4	bay leaves
1	teaspoon Worcestershire sauce
½	teaspoon black pepper
1	11-ounce box of quick cooking barley

In a large Dutch Oven, brown beef. Do not drain. Add onions, tomatoes, garlic salt, and basil. Cook over medium heat for 5 minutes. Add remaining ingredients and bring to a boil. Reduce heat. Let simmer at least 10 to 15 minutes. The longer it simmers the more flavorful it gets (I think!) Remove bay leaves before serving.

Serves 24

.2 Fat Grams

Calories: 116

♥ *Acorn Squash Bake* ♥

12	acorn squash
1	cup dark brown sugar
¾	cup lite pancake syrup (maple flavor)
8	ounces fat-free margarine
	(I use Ultra Promise)
½	teaspoon lite salt

Preheat oven to 350 degrees. Cut acorn squash in half and clean seeds out. Bake for 45 minutes. Cool. Scoop out meat of squash in large bowl. Add remaining ingredients and beat with mixer on medium speed until well blended. Keep refrigerated until ready to eat. Microwave for about 5 to 7 minutes or until warm. Serve warm.

♥ "Pink Cadillac" Jello Salad ♥

Serves 13

0 Fat Grams

Calories: 52

1 20-ounce can of crushed pineapple in its juice
1 box of strawberry sugar-free Jello
   (4 servings size)
1 cup fat-free cottage cheese
1 cup Cool Whip Free
1 fresh strawberry to garnish, if desired

In a saucepan, heat crushed pineapple to a boil. Add strawberry Jello. Remove from heat and stir well. Cool. Then add cottage cheese and Cool Whip. Pour into medium-size serving bowl.

Make three cuts halfway through the fresh strawberry and with fingers, open strawberry into a fan shape. Place on top of Jello for a pretty garnish.

♥ Mashed Potato Bake ♥

Serves 15

0 Fat Grams

Calories: 65

6   cups boiled potatoes, peeled and cubed
12 ounces fat-free cottage cheese
1   envelope Butter Buds
1   small onion, finely chopped (½ cup)
1   teaspoon lite salt (optional)
1   Tablespoon chopped parsley (optional)
    Pepper to taste (optional)

Preheat oven to 350 degrees. In medium-size bowl, beat all ingredients with mixer on medium high for 3 to 4 minutes. Spray a 9 x 13-inch pan with a non-fat cooking spray. Bake for 30 to 35 minutes. Top may be lightly browned.

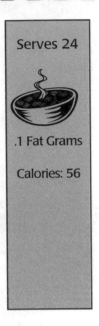

Serves 24

.1 Fat Grams

Calories: 56

♥ *Cream of Mushroom &* *Broccoli Soup* ♥

2	bunches fresh broccoli, chopped
	(OR a 2-pound bag frozen broccoli)
1½	cups grated carrots
4	cups fresh mushrooms, thinly sliced
2	onions, chopped
2	packages Butter Buds, dry
1	Tablespoon garlic salt
¼	teaspoon pepper
3	quarts skim milk
1	cup cornstarch
8	ounces fat-free shredded cheddar cheese
16	ounces fat-free plain yogurt
1	Tablespoon lite salt

Cook broccoli and carrots in microwave until tender. In large saucepan, sauté onions and mushrooms over low-medium heat with dry Butter Buds, garlic salt, lite salt, and pepper for about 5 minutes on low heat until onions are tender. Add broccoli and carrots. Sauté 15 minutes. Mix milk and cornstarch together. Slowly stir into soup. Add yogurt and cheddar cheese, simmer until thickened, about ½ hour. Make sure the heat is not too hot, the soup could easily scorch.

If you don't want to pucker, don't eat sour lemons.

♥ *Carrot & Lentil Soup* ♥

A hearty, stick to your bones, high protein and fiber soup!!!

1	**pound lentils**
8	**cups water**
4	**cups sliced carrots**
1	**medium onion, finely chopped**
1	**46-ounce can of V-8 Juice**
1	**28-ounce can crushed tomatoes, concentrated**
1	**teaspoon Liquid Smoke-Hickory Seasoning** (found in Bar-B-Que sauce section of grocery store)
2	**bay leaves**
1	**Tablespoon plus 1 teaspoon garlic salt**
2	**teaspoons NutraSweet Spoonful** (OR 1½ **Tablespoons sugar**)

Serves 19

.61 Fat Grams

With
Nutraweet —
Calories: 121
With sugar —
Calories: 123

In large saucepan, bring lentils and water to a rapid boil; boil for 2 minutes. Reduce heat to a simmer. Add remaining ingredients. Cover and simmer for at least two hours (until carrots and lentils are tender). Stir occasionally.

♥ *French Fries — The Healthy Ones* ♥

My daughters love eating these fries! They compare restaurant fries to mine and nine times out of ten they say, "Those fries were okay, but not as good as yours, Mom!"

4	**potatoes — your favorite type of potato**
	Non-fat cooking spray
	Lawry's seasoning salt

Serves 4

2 Fat Grams

Preheat oven to 350 degrees. Cut potatoes into long strips, about ¼-inch thick. Spray cookie sheet with non-fat cooking spray, and place strips on sheet. Do not let edges touch each other! Spray tops with non-fat cooking spray and lightly sprinkle with Lawry's seasoning salt. Bake for 20 minutes, then turn fries over. Spray with non-fat cooking spray and bake another 15 to 20 minutes. Fries will be crispy and golden when done. * Note: The calories would be the same as eating a baked potato, except for the non-fat cooking spray you use. So use it sparingly!

Serves 14

3.64 Fat Grams

Calories: 201

♥ *Chicken Poppie Soup* ♥

1	**pound raw skinless chicken breast, cut into bite-sized pieces**
1	**6-ounce box stuffing mix, chicken flavor**
1	**packet Butter Buds, dry**
2	**cups water**
1	**.25 ounce box Knorr Vegetable Soup Mix, dry**
1	**46-ounce can clear chicken broth** (Remove fat floating on top of broth)
2½-3	**cups flour**
46	**ounces water** (Fill empty chicken broth can once)

In a large bowl add 2 cups water to Stove Top Stuffing Mix (croutons and seasoning packet) along with Butter Buds and stir. Set aside. In large saucepan cook raw chicken, chicken broth, vegetable soup mix, and 46 ounces water over medium high heat. Bring to a boil.

While soup is coming to a boil add 1½ cups of flour to stuffing, ½ cup at a time. Mix together well. Place stuffing mixture on floured surface. Sprinkle flour on top of stuffing so that you can press dough out into ½ -inch thickness. With knife cut dough into ¾ to 1-inch pieces. Drop cut dough pieces into boiling soup. Let boil 7 minutes. Dough pieces will be thoroughly cooked and kind of stiff when done. Serve hot.

♥ *My Mom's Au Gratin Soup* ♥

Easy to put together and absolutely delicious!

3   boxes Au Gratin potatoes (your favorite brand), set cheese aside
1   head fresh cauliflower
1   bunch broccoli
1   packet onion soup mix, dry
1½   quarts skim milk
1   teaspoon rubbed thyme, dried
1   teaspoon marjoram leaves, dried
2   teaspoons parsley
3   packets of cheese from the boxed potatoes
8   slices fat-free American cheese
2   teaspoons cornstarch (optional)
     Salt to taste
     Pepper to taste

Put first four ingredients into a six-quart Dutch Oven. Cover with water (approximately 4½ quarts), until all ingredients are covered. Bring to a boil, reduce heat, and simmer until tender, about 20 to 30 minutes. Add remaining ingredients and simmer 5 minutes or until cheese is melted.

If it's not as thick as you would like it, add 2 teaspoons cornstarch with ¼ cup milk.

Thinly chopped turkey ham can be added for variety.

Serves 7

0 Fat Grams

Calories: 21

♥ *Orange Cranberry Jello Salad* ♥

1	cup boiling water
1	4-serving sized orange Jello, sugar-free
1	16-ounce can jellied cranberry sauce
1	4-ounce can Mandarin oranges, drained

Add 1 cup boiling water to Jello. Stir for 2 minutes. Add jellied cranberry sauce, stir. Once dissolved, add oranges. Refrigerate at least 2 hours or overnight. Serve chilled.

Serves 24

.1 Fat Grams

Calories: 29

♥ *Honey Dijon Salad Dressing* ♥

Excellent for potato salad and also "Summer Fiesta! Salad."

¼	cup honey
¼	cup brown sugar
½	cup plus 2 teaspoons water
¾	cup Kraft Free Miracle Whip
¾	cup Kraft Free Mayonnaise
¼	cup Dijon mustard
⅓	cup apple cider vinegar
1	teaspoon garlic salt

In a microwave safe bowl heat honey, brown sugar, and water until dissolved, approximately 30 seconds. Add remaining ingredients. Beat on high with blender until thoroughly mixed.

♥ *Crunchy Sunshine Salad* ♥

As a child this was my favorite Jello salad.

1   **8-serving sized box orange flavored sugar-free Jello**
1½   **cups boiling water**
1   **cup diet Sprite**
¾   **cup finely chopped fresh carrots**
¾   **cup finely chopped fresh celery**
¼   **cup finely chopped pecans** (or walnuts)
1   **20-ounce can crushed pineapple** (drain juice!)
1   **cup no-fat ricotta cheese** (I like Frigo)
1   **11-ounce can Mandarin orange segments, drained** (optional)

Serves 9

2.25 Fat Grams

Calories: 95 per serving (with oranges)

In large bowl, dissolve Jello with boiling water. Stir for 2 minutes. Add diet Sprite, carrots, celery, pecans, drained pineapple and no-fat ricotta cheese. Stir until ricotta cheese is almost completely smooth. Pour into individual glass cups, a pretty jello mold, or a pretty bowl. Refrigerate about 1 hour until firm. Arrange orange segments in flowers on top of Jello before serving.

If you don't have pretty dessert cups, spoon into wine glasses, for a special treat.

Remember, our actions speak louder than our words.

♥♥♥

Serves 8-10

♥ *Chicken Caesar Salad* ♥

This is by far my family's favorite salad!!!

2   **heads Romaine lettuce, cleaned and torn into bite-sized pieces**
1   **cup fat-free Caesar Dressing (I like Hidden Valley's)**
4   **chicken breasts**
½   **cup finely shredded Parmesan cheese**
    Pepper (optional)
    Fat-free croutons (optional)

In large bowl, toss lettuce with Caesar dressing. Cook chicken breasts on grill. Slice into thin strips. Divide salad onto 4 plates. Top with chicken strips. Garnish with shredded Parmesan cheese, fat-free croutons and ground pepper. Best when salad is chilled and chicken is hot off the grill. This salad is also excellent without the chicken.

♥ *Cinnamon Apple Salad* ♥

Serves 8

0 Fat Grams

Calories: 42

A dessert or a side dish. This recipe is especially good with chicken or pork meals.

1   **teaspoon cinnamon**
1   **4-serving sized box sugar-free strawberry Jello**
1   **cup hot water**
1   **cup applesauce**
1   **cup finely chopped apple, with skin on**
1   **cup chopped celery**

Dissolve Jello and cinnamon in hot water, stirring constantly until completely dissolved. Add applesauce and stir until completely mixed. Stir in apples and celery. Once well mixed, pour into Jello ring mold, if desired. Chill at least 2 hours.

♥ *Vegetable Jello Salad* ♥

Serves 15

This recipe is a sneaky way to make sure your children eat their vegetables!
This vegetable Jello salad is great with chicken!

4	**cups water**
1	**can crushed pineapple in its own juice**
1	**4-serving sized box lemon sugar-free Jello**
1	**4-serving sized box orange sugar-free Jello**
1	**cup finely-chopped celery**
1	**teaspoon vinegar**
	(I use apple cider vinegar)
2	**cups shredded carrots**
8	**Tablespoons Kraft Free Miracle Whip**

0 Fat Grams

Calories: 41

In saucepan bring water and pineapple, with juice, to a boil.
Remove from heat. Add both lemon and orange jello. Let cool
a couple of minutes. Add celery, vinegar, and carrots. Pour
into a 9 x 13-inch pan. Let sit at least 4 hours or overnight. With a
knife smooth on Free Miracle Whip before serving.

♥ *Large Shrimp Sunshine Salad* ♥

Serves 1

Calories: 320

	3-4 cups your favorite lettuces, cleaned and cut into bite-sized pieces
½	**cup Marzetti Fat-free Sweet and Sour Salad Dressing**
1	**cup salad shrimp, cooked and chilled**
¼	**cup pineapple chunks, drained**
¼	**cup grated carrots**

Toss all ingredients together. Serve chilled.

2.5 Fat Grams

With
NutraSweet—
Calories: 96
With sugar —
Calories: 97

♥ *California Sunshine Salad* ♥

1   pound cooked spaghetti, drained and cooled

10   slices honey roasted and smoked turkey breast lunch meat, diced

1   pound California blend frozen vegetables, thawed (carrots, broccoli, and cauliflower)

1   medium sweet onion, chopped
     Salt
     Pepper

Combine all ingredients in large bowl. Salt and pepper to taste.

Dressing:

½   cup rice vinegar

1   teaspoon NutraSweet Spoonful (OR 1 teaspoon sugar)

2   teaspoons ginger

⅓   cup water

½   teaspoon poppy seed

Mix dressing ingredients all together. Pour over salad. Serve chilled.

♥ Grilled Steak and Salad ♥

This is a meal in itself! Serve with your favorite fat-free salad dressing.

3   **cups of your favorite lettuces**
1   **hard boiled egg white, chopped**
¼   **cup chopped onions**
¼   **cup chopped mushrooms, fresh**
3-4 **ounces eye of round** (beef)
     Garlic Salt (optional)
     Your favorite fat-free dressing

In large bowl, combine lettuce, egg white, onions, and mushrooms. Set aside. Grill beef to desired doneness. Slice into ¼-inch slices while still hot. Sprinkle with garlic salt lightly. Arrange steak on salad. Top with dressing as desired.

Serves 1

4.6 Fat Grams

Calories: 169 per serving (without dressing)

♥ Festive Cranberry Pineapple Salad ♥

Great for the holidays with turkey or ham.

12   **ounces fresh cranberries**
½   **cup NutraSweet Spoonful** (OR ½ cup sugar)
1   **8-ounce carton Cool Whip Free**
2   **cups miniature marshmallows**
¼   **cup chopped walnuts** (optional)
1   **20-ounce can crushed pineapple, drained**

Grind cranberries in food processor for 1 minute. Pour into bowl and add remaining ingredients. Keep chilled at least 6 hours. The longer it sits the better I think it tastes.

Serves 14

1 Fat Gram

With NutraSweet — Calories: 105
With sugar — Calories: 133

♥ *Kermit's Salad* ♥

Serves 12

.4 Fat Grams

Calories: 38

This is a tart salad.

1	**4-serving sized box sugar-free lime Jello**
1	**4-serving sized box sugar-free lemon Jello**
1	**cup hot water**
2	**cups diet Mountain Dew**
1	**can crushed pineapple in its juice, drained**
1	**cup Free Miracle Whip**
1	**cup fat-free cottage cheese**
1	**Tablespoon finely-chopped pecans** (optional)

Dissolve both Jellos in hot water. Once completely dissolved, stir in Mountain Dew. Set aside. In separate bowl, combine pineapple, Miracle Whip, and cottage cheese. Once well blended, add to Jello. Refrigerate at least 3 hours before serving. Sprinkle with finely-chopped nuts, if desired.

♥ *Gourmet Chicken Salad* ♥

This is my absolute best!

Serves 4

3.25 Fat Grams

Calories: 169

1	**Tablespoon chopped chives**
½	**cup fat-free Miracle Whip**
2	**teaspoons sesame seeds**
2	**teaspoons lemon juice** (I use bottled lemon juice)
2	**teaspoons brown sugar**
2	**teaspoons ground ginger** Dash of lite salt (optional)
2	**cups cooked boneless chicken breast, cubed** (approximately 10 oz.)
½	**cup apples with skin on, coarsely chopped** (1 small)
25	**raisins, chopped**
¼	**cup coarsely chopped celery**

Mix chives, Miracle Whip, sesame seeds, lemon juice, brown sugar, ginger and lite salt, in a medium-large bowl. Mix until well blended. Add chicken breast, apples, raisins, and celery. Toss until well covered with dressing. Cover and keep refrigerated until ready to eat.

Different ways to serve Gourmet Chicken Salad:

*Use ½ of a cantaloupe or honeydew melon. Cut melon in half. With spoon clean out seeds. With knife cut the end of the melon flat giving the bowl shape a flat surface to sit on. Stuff melon with gourmet chicken salad.

*Take a seedless Navel orange and cut into 8 slices, not cutting all the way through. Open like a flower. Stuff center of opened up flower cut orange with gourmet chicken salad.

*Serve gourmet chicken salad on top of a pretty bed of assorted freshly torn lettuce leaves.

*Serve open faced on half a toasted raisin bagel.

*Serve on top of chilled pasta.

♥ *Di's Zingy Italian Pasta* ♥

Serves 10

.5 Fat Grams

Calories: 50

8	ounces spiral pasta, cooked in unsalted water and drained
2	medium tomatoes, cut into wedges
1	cucumber, peeled and diced
1	green pepper, diced
½	cup fat-free Miracle Whip
⅓	cup red wine vinegar (I use a little less than 1/2 cup)
1	Tablespoon + ½ teaspoon sugar
2	Tablespoons + 1 teaspoon dry Italian Seasoning Mix

In a large bowl, combine pasta, tomatoes, cucumber, and green pepper. Set aside. In a separate bowl, combine Miracle Whip, vinegar, sugar, and seasoning mix. Taste this mixture and adjust it to your taste. Pour over salad and toss to coat well. Cover and chill two hours.

♥ *Tuna-Pasta Salad Delight* ♥

Serves 6

1.1 Fat Grams

Calories: 348

1	6 ounce-can tuna (in water)
½	medium onion, chopped
8	slices no-fat American cheese, sliced into thin strips
3	egg whites, hard boiled, chopped
12	ounces rotini pasta, cooked, drained, and rinsed with cold water
2	8-ounce bottles of fat-free Thousand Island salad dressing (I use HiddenValley)

In a large bowl, combine tuna, onion, cheese and egg whites. Stir in dressing, and toss with pasta. Chill.

Great served chilled in half of a cantaloupe! Cut bottom of melons off to make a bowl out of the cantaloupe.

♥ *Taco Salad* ♥

This is a very hearty, stick-to-your-bones salad! Eat as a meal or a side dish.

Serves 6

3.16 Fat Grams

Calories: 243

1	**pound ground eye of round** (beef)
1	**envelope taco seasoning mix**
¾	**cup water**
2	**large heads of iceberg lettuce, torn into bite-sized pieces**
8	**ounces fat-free shredded cheddar cheese**
4	**fresh tomatoes, diced**
1	**medium onion, chopped**
8	**ounces fat-free Western salad dressing** (Use more if desired)
48	**low-fat tortilla chips, crushed**

Brown hamburger. Drain any juices. Add taco seasoning mix and water. Bring to a boil. Reduce heat. Simmer for 15 minutes. Remove from heat. Set aside to cool.

In a very large bowl toss lettuce with cheese, tomatoes, and onion. Toss the seasoned taco meat, tortilla chips, salad dressing, and sour cream in salad right before serving. You don't want to put the last four ingredients in salad too soon before eating or lettuce will become wilted and tortilla chips will become soggy.

If desired you can use the seasoned taco meat warmed or cooled. I would encourage you NOT to put the meat in warm, unless you are going to eat the salad immediately.

This is excellent served as a meal!

One of the greatest lessons we can teach our children is to be responsible for their actions.

♥♥♥

♥ *Seafood Chowder* ♥

This is a special treat anytime! Use as an appetizer or as a main meal!
Excellent!

1	**14.5-ounce can chicken broth**
⅓	**cup shredded carrots**
1	**envelope Butter Buds, dry**
1	**Tablespoon garlic salt** (optional)
¾	**cup sliced mushrooms**
½	**cup chopped onion**
½	**teaspoon thyme** (**Rub between palms of hands before putting in to make fine**)
1	**pound shrimp, cleaned** (**If using medium or large size, cut in half lengthwise**)
1	**10-ounce can baby clams, with juice**
3	**cups skim milk**
4	**Tablespoons flour**
8	**ounces crab meat, cut into bite-sized pieces** (**Imitation may be used**)
	Dash of pepper (optional)

In Dutch Oven or large saucepan, combine chicken broth, carrots,
Butter Buds, garlic salt, mushrooms, onions, and thyme. Bring to a
boil. Reduce heat to a very low simmer. Add shrimp, clams with
juice, and crab meat. Stir in 2 cups of milk. Add flour to remaining
cup of milk. Quickly stir until flour is dissolved. Pour into
chowder. Stir for about 5 minutes until
thick and creamy. Serve hot.

*In order to
shine, some of
us need more
polishing than
others.*

♥ *Broccoli & Potato Casserole* ♥

If you like twice-baked potatoes, you'll like this!

Serves 12

.3 Fat Grams

Calories: 130

8   **medium potatoes** (approximately 2 pounds)
1   **9-ounce package of fat-free herb dressing mix** (I use Good Seasons)
1   **package reduced-calorie ranch dressing mix** (I use Hidden Valley)
2   **cups skim milk**
¼   **cup fat-free sour cream**
1   **16-ounce bag of frozen broccoli**
4   **ounces fat-free margarine** (I use Ultra Promise)
1   **cup crushed Frito Lay Baked Low-Fat Potato Chips**

Bake potatoes until tender. Once the potatoes are cooled, peel off the skins with your fingers. Discard skins. Put peeled potatoes in large bowl. Add both salad dressing packets, milk, margarine, and sour cream to potatoes. Break potatoes up enough so that the mixer will work smoothly. Beat on medium for about 1½ to 2 minutes. It will be creamy with some lumps in it. Set aside. Cook broccoli in microwave as directed on package. Drain water. With large spoon gently mix broccoli with potato mixture.

Preheat oven to 350 degrees. Spray a 9 x 13-inch pan with non-fat cooking spray. Put potato-broccoli mixture in pan and bake for ½ hour. Remove from oven and increase oven temperature to 450 degrees. Crush potato chips to make 1 cup. Sprinkle over potato-broccoli mixture. Put back in oven for 1½ to 2 minutes. Broil until top is toasty brown. Serve warm.

Cooking Hint: What I'd encourage you to do if you're having baked potatoes, make about 2 pounds more (approximately 8 medium to small potatoes) and keep in the refrigerator until ready to make this recipe.

Main Dishes

&

Casseroles

Mini Contents
Main Dishes &
Casseroles

♥ *Teriyaki Chicken Kebobs* ♥

This dish is excellent served with my Seasoned Rice!

Kebob ingredients:

2   **pounds boneless, skinless chicken breast, cut into 1-1½-inch chunks**
8   **kebob stick skewers**
1   **whole fresh pineapple, cleaned, and cut into ½-1-inch chunks**
3-4 **medium sweet onions, cut into eighths**
2   **fresh green peppers, cut into eighths**
2   **fresh red peppers, cut into eighths**

Marinade sauce:

1   **cup pineapple juice**
1   **cup lite teriyaki marinade sauce or lite soy sauce** (Either one; LaChoy makes both)
½   **teaspoon ground ginger**
½   **teaspoon garlic powder**
2-3 **Tablespoons cornstarch**

Marinate cut-up chicken pieces at least 2 to 3 hours before serving. (Chicken can also be marinated a day or two in advance.). Preheat oven to 350 degrees. Place chicken pieces, pineapple, onion, and peppers on skewers. Pour marinade over chicken kebobs and cook in any manner you desire for 15 to 20 minutes or until fully done.

After cooking, drain marinade into medium saucepan. Add 2 to 3 Tablespoons cornstarch and cook over medium-low heat, stirring constantly until smooth and creamy.

If desired, serve chicken kebobs on a bed of seasoned rice. Pour 2 Tablespoons of marinade sauce over each kebob and rice. Remaining sauce can be served in a side dish for dipping chicken.

♥ *Fried Chicken Strips* ♥

Great served plain or with your favorite fat-free salad dressing as a dip.

¾	**cup toasted bread crumbs**
¼	**cup whole wheat flour**
2	**teaspoons garlic salt**
¼	**teaspoon ground black pepper**
1	**Tablespoon grated Parmesan cheese**
4	**egg whites**
⅓	**cup skim milk**
1	**pound boneless, skinless chicken breast, with all visible fat removed. Cut into long strips ½-inch wide.**

Preheat oven to 400 degrees. Spray cookie sheet with non-fat cooking spray. Mix together first five ingredients. Set aside. Whip egg whites and milk together with whisk or beater for 1 minute. One at a time, dip chicken strips into egg mixture. Drain off excess, then dip in bread crumb mixture. Repeat this process, dipping each chicken strip a second time into the egg mixture, and then the crumb mixture.

Place prepared chicken strips on cookie sheet and spray chicken strips with non-fat cooking spray. Bake for 8 to 10 minutes. Turn over and bake an additional 7 to 10 minutes. Bottoms will be golden brown when ready to turn.

Stay focused on all that is good, right, and true.

♥♥♥

♥ *Sweet & Sassy Meatballs* ♥

Easy! These are always a big hit! Serve as an appetizer or entree.

Meatballs:

3   egg whites
1   pound ground eye of round (beef)
½   cup bread crumbs
1   small onion, finely chopped
¼   teaspoon lite salt
¼   teaspoon pepper

Beat egg whites with fork. Add remaining ingredients and mix until well blended. Measuring carefully, take 1 Tablespoon of meat mixture, and roll into ball with hands. Repeat the procedure with remaining mixture. Makes approximately 25 meatballs.

Sauce:

1   8-ounce can tomato sauce
¾   cup ketchup
¼   cup firmly packed brown sugar (lite or dark)
2   Tablespoons NutraSweet Spoonful (OR 2 Tablespoons sugar)

Preheat oven to 350 degrees. For easier cleanup, cover cookie sheet or jelly roll pan with foil. Spray with a non-fat cooking spray. Mix all ingredients with fork, until sauce is well blended. Dip each meatball completely in sauce. Place meatballs on foil. Bake for 30 minutes.

* With tongs, dip each meatball (once again) completely into sauce. Place meatballs back onto foiled sheet and return to oven for 15 minutes. Serve immediately.

*For easier dipping of the meatballs, pour the sauce (once made) into a cup.

♥ *Oriental Teriyaki Beef Dinner* ♥

This meal is a huge hit with our children.

Serves 4

6.75 Fat Grams

Calories: 304

1   **20-ounce can pineapple chunks in juice or 1/2 cup pineapple juice**

½   **cup lite teriyaki marinade sauce** (I use LaChoy)

¼   **teaspoon ground ginger**

¼   **teaspoon garlic powder**

1   **pound eye of round beef cut into 1⅓-inch cubes** (all visible fat removed)

1   **medium to small onion cut into eighths** (separate layers of onion)

4   **cups frozen stir fry vegetables** (oriental mixture with pea pods)

2   **Tablespoons cornstarch**

Drain juice from pineapple, retaining juice. In medium bowl, combine teriyaki marinade, pineapple juice, ground ginger, and garlic powder. Mix well until ginger and garlic are completely dissolved. Add beef and onion. Cover tightly and refrigerate, at least 15 minutes. (The longer this marinates, the more flavorful the beef becomes. This can be done days in advance, if desired.)

Drain marinade and set aside. Use either a wok or large pan. Spray pan with a non-fat cooking spray. Cook meat and onions over medium heat for about 5 minutes before adding frozen vegetables. Add 2 Tablespoons cornstarch to marinade and mix well until cornstarch is completely dissolved. Pour marinade over meat and vegetables being cooked. Stir and bring to a boil. Cook for about 5 minutes or until vegetables are slightly crisp, yet tender.

♥ 3-in-1 Chicken Vegetable Soup ♥

This is a hearty, down home, good eatin' country soup that's delicious...even in the suburbs and cities! These aren't just soups — they're meals!

Once the main soup has been prepared, you have your choice; I like to make at least one other soup from the main base of this wonderful chicken vegetable soup. Follow these simple directions:

(Main Recipe)

Chicken Vegetable Soup:

14	cups water
4	chicken-flavored bouillon cubes
4	whole bay leaves
1	15- to 16-ounce can spinach
1	15- to 16-ounce can asparagus
1	15- to 16-ounce can sliced stewed tomatoes
1	15- to 16-ounce can creamed corn
1	16-ounce bag of frozen oriental-style mixed vegetables
1	16-ounce bag of frozen mixed vegetables
1	teaspoon sweet basil
½	teaspoon black pepper
1	Tablespoon garlic powder
1	Tablespoon garlic salt
2½ -3	cups chicken breast (approximately 3 10-ounce chicken breasts)

Bring chicken to boil in water. (If not using boneless chicken, boil for about 5 minutes. Remove chicken from water, and debone, if necessary.) Remove fat from chicken water by pouring chicken water through a strainer filled with ice positioned over a large pot. The ice will collect the fat from the water. If needed, this process can be repeated 2 or 3 times. Add remaining ingredients to chicken water. Once again, bring to a boil.

If you wish, you can now make 2 of the 3 recipes from this main soup.

(1)   *Chicken Vegetable Soup* — It's all done now except the eatin'.

(2)   *Chicken Noodle Vegetable Soup* — Take half the recipe, and add 2 additional cups of water. Bring to a boil. Add 12-ounce bag noodles. (For lower fat intake, use "No Yolks" noodles.) Stir vigorously until soup boils again (approximately 30 seconds). Boil for 6 to 7 minutes. Serve hot.

(3)   *Chicken Rice Vegetable Soup* — Add 1 cup long grain rice to half the main recipe — chicken vegetable soup. Bring to a boil, reduce heat, cover tightly, and simmer for 20 minutes. Serve hot.

Very important! Remove bay leaves before eating!

Note: As noted earlier, these are hearty soups. If you like brothier soup, simply add water or canned chicken broth. Campbell's Ready to Serve Chicken Broth is good.

These soups can easily be reheated.

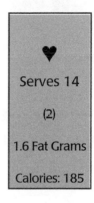

♥

Serves 29

(1)

1.4 Fat Grams

Calories: 89

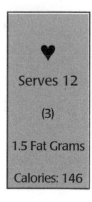

♥

Serves 14

(2)

1.6 Fat Grams

Calories: 185

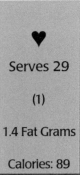

♥

Serves 12

(3)

1.5 Fat Grams

Calories: 146

♥ *2 Dinners in One Roast* ♥

This can serve 12 at 298 calories (¼ pound beef each) or eat half of this recipe and save the rest for stew.

♥ *Meal #1 — Pot Roast* ♥

2	**cups water**
1	**package dry onion soup mix** (approximately 1.37 oz.)
3	**pounds eye of round** (beef), **with all visible fat trimmed off**
12	**potatoes, cut in eighths**
8	**medium onions, cut into eighths**
2	**pounds fresh carrots, peeled and cut in 3 - 4-inch lengths**

Preheat oven to 375 degrees. In large Dutch Oven or roaster pan, add water and dry soup mix , stirring until soup is dissolved. Put in roast, then add remaining ingredients, in this order, on top of roast: potatoes, onions, carrots. Bake for 3 hours or put in Crock-Pot on medium heat for 4 to 5 hours. Eat half of this prepared meal. Save second half, including juices, and refrigerate until needed (See following recipe.).

♥ *Meal #2 — Stew* ♥

Serves 12

3 Fat Grams

Calories: 185

Use ½ prepared leftover juices and onion soup from Meal #1 and add:

4   **cups skim milk**
2   **cups cornstarch**
⅛   **teaspoon ground black pepper**
¼   **teaspoon dried basil**
1   **teaspoon A-1 Sauce**
1   **16-ounce can sweet peas, drained**
1   **teaspoon lite salt**

Chop leftover eye of round roast into small bite-sized pieces. Drain onion soup from Meal #1 into two-quart saucepan. Add 3 cups milk and warm on medium-low heat. In bowl, combine remaining 1 cup milk with 1 cup cornstarch. Stir until cornstarch is completely dissolved. Add milk-cornstarch mixture to milk-soup mixture. Add all seasonings and A-1 Sauce. Stir constantly until gravy is thick and creamy.

Pour gravy over potatoes, onions, cut-up roast, and carrots. Add peas. Stir until completely covered with gravy. Cover and keep refrigerated for up to 5 days. Just heat before serving. If desired, the second meal can be frozen until ready to use.

♥ *"Seconds Please" Meatloaf* ♥

Serves 8

3.2 Fat Grams

With Equal —
Calories: 187
With Sugar —
Calories: 217

14-16	ounces Healthy Choice smoked sausage
1	pound ground eye of round (beef)
¾	cup Italian seasoned bread crumbs
1	medium onion, chopped
1	small green pepper, chopped
½	teaspoon salt, optional
½	teaspoon pepper
2	egg whites, beaten

Topping:

½	cup ketchup
1	8-ounce can tomato sauce
⅓	cup brown sugar
8	packets of Equal (OR 1/3 cup sugar)

Preheat oven to 350 degrees. Grind smoked sausage in food processor or blender. In large bowl, add all ingredients and mix well. For easier cleanup, cover a jelly roll pan (a cookie sheet with edges) with foil. Spray with a non-fat cooking spray. With hands, shape meatloaf mixture into a loaf. Bake for 35-40 minutes.

While meatloaf is baking, mix topping ingredients in medium-sized bowl. Spoon mixture over meatloaf. Return to oven and bake an additional ½ hour.

If you want to give yourself a dose of good medicine, do something for someone else — for no other reason than to bless them.

♥♥♥

♥ *Creamy Macaroni & Cheese* ♥

Serves 8

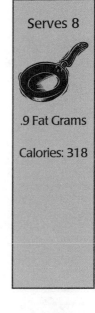

.9 Fat Grams

Calories: 318

16   ounces large pasta shells, boiled and drained

16   ounces fat-free sharp cheese, cut into small pieces

2   ounces fat-free shredded cheddar cheese

1   12-ounce can of lite evaporated skimmed milk

½   teaspoon lite salt (optional)

Cook and drain pasta as directed on box. In same pan, add both cheeses and evaporated milk over low heat on stove. Add salt. Serve warm immediately.

♥ *Baked Vermicelli* ♥

Serves 12

2.3 Fat Grams

Calories: 270

1   pound ground eye of round (beef)

½   teaspoon ground sage

1   30-ounce jar of your favorite spaghetti sauce (I use Healthy Choice)

1   16-ounce box vermicelli

20   ounces fat-free ricotta cheese

2   Tablespoons grated Parmesan cheese

8   ounces fat-free mozzarella cheese

16   ounces vermicelli

Preheat oven to 350 degrees. Spray 9 x 13-inch baking pan with non-fat cooking spray. In large pan, brown beef with sage. Add spaghetti sauce to hamburger. Turn off heat. Cook vermicelli as directed on package, drain water. Stir cooked vermicelli with spaghetti sauce. Pour vermicelli with sauce into prepared pan. Spread ricotta cheese on top. Sprinkle with Parmesan, then add mozzarella cheese on top of Parmesan. Bake for 30 minutes.

This dish can be prepared in advance and frozen (up to 4 weeks) or refrigerated (up to 3 days). Bake 15-20 minutes longer if taken directly from the freezer.

♥ *Cheesy Tuna Casserole* ♥

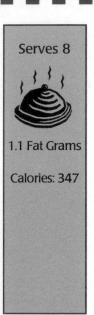

Serves 8

1.1 Fat Grams

Calories: 347

16 ounces large pasta shells, boiled for 13 minutes and drained
16 ounces fat-free sharp cheese, cut into small pieces
2 ounces fat-free shredded cheddar cheese
1 12-ounce can lite evaporated milk
1 6-ounce can tuna in water
1 4-ounce can mushroom pieces
½ teaspoon salt (optional)

Cook and drain pasta as directed on box. In same pan add both cheeses and evaporated milk over low heat on stove. Add tuna, mushrooms and salt. Serve warm immediately.

♥ *Thick Chili* ♥

Serves 16

5.6 Fat Grams

Calories: 203

3 pounds ground eye of round (beef)
2 onions, chopped
2 Tablespoons water
½ teaspoon chili powder
1 31-ounce can Brooks Chili Hot Beans in Chili Sauce
1 16-ounce can stewed tomatoes, sliced
3 6-ounce cans tomato paste
1 8-ounce can tomato sauce
2 teaspoons garlic

Brown beef in large pan. Drain and rinse beef in strainer to eliminate fat. Sauté chopped onion in 2 Tablespoons water until soft. Add browned beef, chili powder, and all remaining ingredients. Mix well. Simmer 10-15 minutes. Serve warm.

♥ *Low-Fat Cheesy Taco Pie* ♥

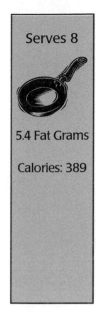

Serves 8

5.4 Fat Grams

Calories: 389

1   14-ounce bag low-fat tortilla chips
4   Tablespoons Molly McButter cheese sprinkles
3-4 Tablespoons water
14 slices fat-free sharp cheddar cheese
    (I use Borden)
1   15¾ ounce can Brooks Chili Hot Beans in Chili Sauce
1   pound ground eye of round (beef)
1   1¼-ounce package taco seasoning mix
    (I use Ortega)
¾   cup water
2   cups shredded lettuce
1   pint cherry tomatoes
⅓   cup non-fat sour cream
    (I use Land O Lakes)
    non-fat French salad dressing (I like Henri's)
½   cup salsa

Preheat oven to 350 degrees. Spray a 9-inch pie pan with non-fat cooking spray. With food processor, crumble ½ bag tortilla chips with 4 Tablespoons Molly McButter cheese sprinkles (reserve ½ cup). Add 3 Tablespoons water to crumb mixture and press into pie pan to form the crust. Lay 4 slices fat-free cheese on crust. Corners of cheese will show.

Combine 6 slices fat-free cheese and Brooks Chili Hot Beans. Blend for 15-20 seconds. Pour ¾ of mixture on top of cheese slices (reserve ¼ cup). Using a spoon, press the mixture onto the sides of the pie pan and up the edges to the top.

Brown and drain beef. Add taco seasoning and ¾ cup water. Simmer 15 minutes on low heat. Pour taco meat over bean mixture. Lay 4 slices of fat-free cheese on top of taco meat. Sprinkle reserved crumb mixture over taco meat. Bake for 30 minutes. Place shredded lettuce on top of warm pie. Top with cherry tomatoes, then non-fat sour cream and drizzle non-fat French salad dressing. Serve warm immediately.

Add ½ cup salsa to reserved ¼ cup bean and cheese mixture. Warm in microwave for 1½ - 2 minutes. Serve as dip with the remaining tortilla chips.

Without the Down Home Fat ♥   **155**

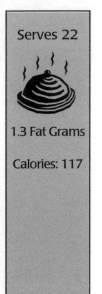
♥ *Chili Mac* ♥

4	**pounds ground eye of round** (beef)
2	**onions, chopped**
2	**Tablespoons water**
½	**teaspoon chili powder**
1	**31-ounce can Brooks Chili Hot Beans in Chili Sauce**
1	**16-ounce can stewed tomatoes, sliced**
3	**6-ounce cans tomato paste**
1	**8-ounce can tomato sauce**
1	**teaspoon garlic**
1	**pound cooked spaghetti or elbow macaroni** **Grated Italian topping** (optional)

Brown beef in large pan. Drain. Using a strainer, rinse beef with cold water to eliminate fat. Cook chopped onion in 2 Tablespoon water until soft. Add browned beef, chili powder, and all remaining ingredients. Mix well. Simmer 10-15 minutes. Sprinkle with grated Italian topping, if desired. Serve warm.

♥ *Spinach Lasagna* ♥

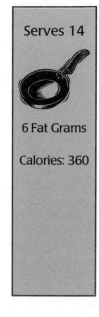

Serves 14

6 Fat Grams

Calories: 360

4   egg whites
2   15-ounce containers fat-free ricotta cheese
1   8-ounce container fat-free sour cream
3   ounces finely shredded Parmesan cheese
¾   cup grated Italian topping (OR grated Parmesan cheese)
2   10-ounce packages frozen chopped spinach — thawed and well-drained
2   26-ounce jars spaghetti sauce with meat (I prefer Healthy Choice)
1   16-ounce box lasagna noodles (use spinach lasagna noodles, if available), cooked
1   pound fat-free mozzarella cheese

Preheat oven to 375 degrees. Spray a 9 x 13-inch and a 7 x 10-inch pan with non-fat cooking spray. Beat egg whites for 30 seconds. Add ricotta cheese, sour cream, Parmesan cheese, grated Italian topping, and spinach. Mix well on medium with mixer.

Put a little spaghetti sauce in bottom of each pan before layering in the following order:

    lasagna noodles
    cheese-spinach mixture
    spaghetti sauce
    mozzarella cheese

Continue to layer in this order until the top of the pan is reached. End with the spaghetti sauce and sprinkle with mozzarella cheese. This recipe will fill both pans. Bake for 45 minutes, then reduce heat to 350 degrees for an additional 15 minutes. Cool 5 minutes before serving.

♥ *Four Cheese Lasagna* ♥

Serves 12

Without spaghetti sauce —
Less than 1 Fat Gram
Calories: 303

With spaghetti sauce —
2 Fat Grams
Calories: 353

4   egg whites
3   8-ounce containers fat-free cottage cheese
1   15-ounce container fat-free ricotta cheese
1   16-ounce box lasagna noodles (prepared as directed on box)
1   pound shredded fat-free Healthy Choice Mexican cheese
1   pound shredded fat-free mozzarella cheese
1   30-ounce jar Prego Three Cheese Spaghetti Sauce (optional)

Preheat oven to 350 degrees. Spray 9 x 13-inch pan with non-fat cooking spray. Beat egg whites with cottage cheese and ricotta cheese for one minute with mixer on high speed. Layer ingredients in the following order:

Lasagna noodles
⅓ cup ricotta and cottage cheese mixture
½ pound Mexican cheese
Lasagna noodles
⅓ cup ricotta and cottage cheese mixture
⅓ pound mozzarella cheese
Lasagna noodles
⅓ cup ricotta and cottage cheese mixture
⅓ pound mozzarella cheese
Lasagna noodles
⅓ pound mozzarella cheese
½ pound Mexican cheese

Bake for 50 minutes. Let cool for a few minutes before cutting.

If desired, warm spaghetti sauce in microwave. When serving, pour ¼ cup of spaghetti sauce over the top of ¹⁄₁₂ portion of baked cheese lasagna.

♥ *Mexican Lasagna* ♥

Serves 12

2 Fat Grams

Calories: 290

If you like spicy foods, you'll like this. It can be made days in advance and refrigerated until needed. After refrigeration, bake for 40-45 minutes rather than 30 minutes.

2   **egg whites**
1   **15-ounce container fat-free ricotta cheese**
      (I use Frigo)
1   **16-ounce box lasagna noodles**
1   **pound ground eye of round** (beef)
1   **package taco seasoning mix** (1¼-ounce size)
1   **pound fat-free shredded cheddar cheese**
      (I prefer the fancy shredded cheese by Healthy
      Choice)
1   **28-ounce jar chunky salsa**
      (Use your favorite brand!)

Preheat oven to 350 degrees. Spray 9 x 13-inch pan with non-fat cooking spray. Beat egg whites with ricotta cheese; set aside. Prepare lasagna noodles as directed on box. Brown hamburger. Drain. Prepare taco seasoning mix with hamburger as directed on back of seasoning package. Layer ingredients in the following order:

> Lasagna noodles
> ⅓ prepared ricotta-cheese mixture, spread thinly over noodles
> All taco-seasoned hamburger
> ⅓ prepared cheddar cheese
> Lasagna noodles
> ½ remaining prepared ricotta-cheese mixture (approximately 5 ounces), spread thinly over noodles
> ½ jar chunky salsa
> ⅓ remainder prepared cheddar cheese
> Lasagna noodles
> Remainder prepared ricotta-cheese mixture
> Remainder chunky salsa
> Remainder cheddar cheese

Bake for ½ hour or until thoroughly warmed.

Serves 12

.66 Fat Grams

Calories: 265

♥ *Vegetable Lasagna* ♥

4	**egg whites**
1	**20-ounce carton fat-free ricotta cheese**
1	**cup fat-free cottage cheese**
1	**packet Butter Buds** (½ ounce), **dry**
1	**teaspoon garlic salt or garlic powder** (whichever you prefer)
6	**cups of your frozen vegetables** (I prefer broccoli, carrots, mushrooms, and onions)
8	**ounces fat-free shredded cheddar cheese** (I use Healthy Choice)
8	**ounces fat-free shredded mozzarella cheese** (I use Healthy Choice)
1	**16-ounce box lasagna noodles**
1	**26-ounce jar of your favorite fat-free spaghetti sauce** (optional)

Preheat oven to 350 degrees. Spray 9 x 13-inch pan with non-fat cooking spray. Beat egg whites, with ricotta cheese, cottage cheese, Butter Buds and garlic salt until well blended. Divide cheese mixture evenly into three bowls. Then add 2 cups frozen vegetables to *each* bowl.

In the first bowl, add 4 ounces shredded cheddar cheese to the cheese and vegetables and mix well. In the second bowl, add 4 ounces shredded mozzarella cheese to the cheese and vegetables and mix well. Layer ingredients in the following order:

> Lasagna noodles
> Mozzarella-vegetable-cheese mixture
> Lasagna noodles
> Cheddar-vegetable-cheese mixture
> Lasagna noodles
> Vegetable-cheese-mixture

Sprinkle remaining shredded mozzarella (approximately 4 ounces) and remaining shredded cheddar (approximately 4 ounces) over lasagna and press into vegetable cheese mixture. Bake for 30 minutes.

Some lasagna noodles may be left over. This dish can be prepared in advance and refrigerated until ready to bake. If desired, microwave your favorite spaghetti sauce and spoon over each serving.

♥ *Lasagna Supreme* ♥

A huge hit for any special occasion!

Serves 12

4.6 Fat Grams

Calories: 343

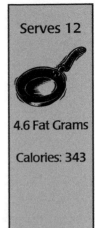

2	egg whites
1	15-ounce container fat-free ricotta cheese (I use Frigo)
14	ounces Healthy Choice Low-fat Smoked Sausage
1	pound ground eye of round (beef)
8	ounces fresh mushrooms — thinly sliced
½	medium onion chopped (approximately ½ cup)
1	27.5-ounce jar — Ragu Today's Chunky Garden Harvest Spaghetti Sauce
1	16-ounce box lasagna — prepared as directed on package
¾	pound fat-free mozzarella cheese (I use Healthy Choice)
6	Tablespoons grated Parmesan cheese

Preheat oven to 350 degrees. Spray a large saucepan and a
9 x 13-inch pan with non-fat cooking spray. Beat egg whites with
ricotta cheese. Set aside. Grind up sausage in food processor. In
prepared saucepan, combine hamburger and sausage until fully
cooked. Do not drain! Add mushrooms and onion. Cover and cook
on low for 4-5 minutes. Add spaghetti sauce. Mix well. Turn off
heat.

Lay 4 long lasagna noodles across the bottom of the prepared
9 x 13-inch pan. The sides of the lasagna noodles will overlap
slightly. Layer the ingredients in the following order:

1½ cups meat sauce

lasagna noodles

1 cup ricotta-cheese mixture

1 cup mozzarella cheese
2 Tablespoons Parmesan cheese, sprinkled
lasagna noodles
1½ cups meat sauce
lasagna noodles
1 cup ricotta-cheese mixture
1 cup mozzarella cheese
2 Tablespoons Parmesan cheese
lasagna noodles
2 cups meat sauce
1 cup mozzarella cheese
2 Tablespoons Parmesan cheese

Note: A little sauce will be left over.

Bake for 30 minutes. Let the dish cool a few minutes before cutting. It can be eaten immediately, refrigerated until ready to use or frozen. (If this dish has been prepared ahead of time and frozen, bake for 45-55 minutes or until it is fully cooked.)

♥ *Steak on a Stick* ♥

Serves 8

5.4 Fat Grams

Calories: 191

Substitute chicken for the steak and have chicken sticks.

2   **pounds eye of round steak** (beef)
1   **21-ounce can crushed pineapple in its own juices**
     Kebob sticks
     Garlic salt (optional)

Cut steak into 1½-inch pieces, removing all visible fat. In Ziploc gallon-sized bag marinate steak pieces in crushed pineapple, and juice, for at least 8 hours. (The longer it marinates, the better I think it tastes.)

Arrange about 6 pieces of steak on kebob stick. Sprinkle lightly with garlic salt. Cook on grill, turning once, until the desired doneness is achieved.

♥ *Breakfast Bake* ♥

Serves 8

1.8 Fat Grams

Calories: 95

2   **drops yellow food coloring**
7   **egg whites**
8   **ounces Healthy Choice Smoked Sausage, thinly sliced**
5   **slices Fat-free Borden Swiss Cheese, cubed**
½   **cup skim milk**
3   **Tablespoons fresh parsley** (optional)
4   **slices fat-free bread, cubed**

Preheat oven to 350 degrees. Spray 9 x 13-inch pan with non-fat cooking spray. Beat 2 drops yellow food coloring and egg whites. Combine all ingredients and pour into prepared pan. Bake for 30-35 minutes.

♥ *Spaghetti Pizza* ♥

Serves 10

1 Fat Gram

Calories: 330

4   **egg whites**
½   **cup skim milk**
1   **cup fat-free mozzarella cheese, shredded**
¾   **teaspoon garlic powder**
½   **teaspoon lite salt** (optional)
1   **pound spaghetti, cooked**

Preheat oven to 350 degrees. Spray a greased jelly roll pan (10 x 15-inch cookie sheet with edges) with non-fat cooking spray. Combine egg whites, skim milk, fat-free shredded mozzarella cheese, garlic powder, and salt. Mix well. Add spaghetti. Pour spaghetti mixture in pan. Bake for 15 minutes.

Topping:
1   **32-ounce jar low-fat spaghetti sauce**
    (I like either Healthy Choice or Ragu's lite brand)
½   **teaspoon oregano**
3   **cups fat-free mozzarella cheese, shredded**
3   **cups of your favorite pizza toppings**
    (chopped onions, green peppers, mushrooms, etc.)

Combine spaghetti sauce and oregano. Spread onto baked spaghetti. Sprinkle on 3 cups of the mozzarella cheese and arrange your favorite pizza toppings on top of cheese. Bake for 30 minutes. Cool 5 minutes before cutting.

God, let me be a living example of Your love.

♥ *Seafood Lasagna* ♥

Definitely an extra special meal for any special occasion!

Seafood Sauce:

1	Tablespoon cornstarch
1	cup cold non-fat buttermilk
1	14.5-ounce can clear chicken broth
2	10-ounce cans whole baby clams
1	packet Butter Buds, dry
½	cup onion, finely chopped
2	teaspoons garlic salt
1	teaspoon thyme (crush with your hands before adding dash of pepper)
	dash of pepper
8	ounces fully cooked crab meat (imitation may be used), cut into bite- sized pieces
1	pound fully cooked shrimp, cleaned and deveined (if shrimp are medium or large, cut in halves lengthwise)

Serves 12

1.25 Fat Grams

Calories: 167

Mix cornstarch with buttermilk until completely dissolved. Place all ingredients in large Dutch Oven over medium-low heat. Bring to boil, stirring often. Remove from heat. With a cup or ladle drain 1½ cups juice from the sauce and reserve for later.

2	egg whites
20	ounces fat-free ricotta cheese
¼	cup bread crumbs — your favorite store brand is fine
3	Tablespoons grated Parmesan cheese
1	16-ounce box lasagna noodles, uncooked
8	ounces fat-free fancy mozzarella cheese, shredded

Preheat oven to 325 degrees. Spray a 9 x 13-inch pan with a non-fat cooking spray. Beat egg whites with ricotta cheese until well blended (about 1 minute). Set aside. Layer the ingredients in the following order:

	Seafood Sauce
5	strips uncooked lasagna
1⅓	cups ricotta-cheese mixture
4	ounces of mozzarella cheese
½	Tablespoon grated Parmesan cheese, sprinkled

5	strips uncooked lasagna noodles
	remainder ricotta-cheese mixture
	remainder Seafood Sauce
	remainder mozzarella
2½	Tablespoons grated Parmesan cheese

Bake for 1 hour.

♥ *Audrey's "Out of This World" Chicken Tenders* ♥

½   **fresh lemon, juiced**
     Lemon and black pepper seasoning
     seasoning salt
1-2 **pounds chicken strips**
     Fat-free Italian dressing

Sprinkle fresh lemon juice, lemon and black pepper seasoning, and seasoned salt on chicken strips. Marinate in Italian dressing for 1-2 days.

Preheat oven to 350 degrees. Spray pan with a non-fat cooking spray. Place chicken strips in prepared pan and bake for 30-45 minutes, turning over once. Remove from oven and place in bowl with a lid, while still hot. Add 2-3 Tablespoons Italian dressing and shake. Chicken is ready to eat and enjoy!

♥ *Carol Strabley's Breakfast Soufflé* ♥

8   **ounces Canadian Bacon**
6   **egg whites**
5   **slices of non-fat bread**
1   **cup non-fat cheddar cheese**
2   **cups skim milk**
1   **teaspoon dry mustard**
   Salt and pepper to taste

Preheat oven to 350 degrees. Spray 9 x 9-inch dish with non-fat cooking spray. Mix all ingredients. Place in dish and refrigerate overnight. Bake for 1 hour or until set.

♥ *Broccoli, Ham, & Cheese Quiche* ♥

Serves 12

1.16 Fat Grams

Calories: 161

Crust:

1	cup buttermilk pancake mix
½	cup + 2 Tablespoons non-fat cream cheese

Preheat oven to 350 degrees. Spray a 9-inch pie pan and an 8-inch cheesecake spring form pan with non-fat cooking spray. Mix non-fat cream cheese and dry pancake mix with mixer on low speed. Mixture will be dry and crumbly. Spray hand with non-fat cooking spray. With sprayed hand divide mixture. Put ⅔ of mixture in prepared pie pan. Using your hand, gently but firmly press dough up the sides of the pie pan to form the crust. Do bottom of pan last. Press with ball of hand to ensure there are no cracks. Do the same to the cheesecake spring form, but do not go up the sides. Two 8- or 9-inch cake pans can be used following the same procedure, but do not go up the sides. Bake the crust for 7 minutes.

Quiche:

12	egg whites
3	drops of yellow food coloring
1	cup fat-free ricotta cheese
½	cup finely chopped onion (approximately 1 small onion)
6	ounces deli thin sliced ham (I use Healthy Choice)
1	4-ounce can sliced mushrooms, drained
2	cups cooked broccoli (If using frozen broccoli, pop it in the microwave and drain it after it is cooked)
1	8-ounce package of fat-free shredded cheese (I use Healthy Choice)

Beat eggs, food coloring, and ricotta cheese together with mixer on medium speed for two minutes. By hand, stir in remaining ingredients. Pour into prepared crust. If using a pie pan, cover sides of crust with foil. Bake for 30-35 minutes. If using a pie pan, remove foil for the last 5 minutes. Serve warm. Great reheated in microwave.

Makes 1 — 9-inch pie pan and 1 — 8-inch cheesecake spring form. Total 2 quiches.

Desserts

Desserts

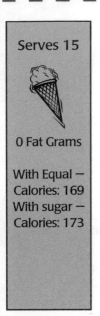

♥ *Strawberry-Banana Trifle* ♥

This needs to be eaten within a day or it gets soggy.

8	**medium-large fresh strawberries, sliced**
2	**packets Equal** (OR 4 teaspoons sugar)
4	**4 serving sized sugar-free pudding mix** (I use D-Zerta)
6	**cups skim milk**
96	**fat-free strawberry wafers** (I use Sunshine)
3	**bananas, sliced**

Toss strawberry slices with Equal and set aside.

Prepare pudding as directed on package, using 6 cups skim milk. Once boiling, remove from heat. Cool 5 minutes, stirring twice.

Lay 48 wafers on bottom of 9 x 13-inch or 10 x 14-inch pan. Arrange bananas on wafers. Spread 1/2 pudding on bananas. Arrange 48 wafers on pudding. Arrange sweetened strawberry slices on wafers. Spread remaining pudding over sliced strawberries. Wrap with film and refrigerate at least 1 hour before serving. Refrigerate unused portions.

♥ *Tropical Baked Rice Dessert* ♥

This is an excellent dessert for someone with ulcers. I like to make extra rice when preparing an oriental dish so that I have it ready to use when preparing this dessert.

10	**egg whites**
½	**Tablespoon coconut extract**
½	**cup brown sugar**
¼	**cup additional brown sugar**
½	**cup skim milk**
4	**cups long-grain enriched rice**
2	**medium bananas, sliced**

Preheat oven to 350 degrees. Spray a 9 x 13-inch pan with a non-fat cooking spray. Beat egg whites with blender on high until foamy. Add coconut extract, ½ cup brown sugar, and skim milk. Beat until well blended. Add rice and beat until well blended. With spoon stir in bananas. Pour mixture into prepared pan and bake for 30 minutes. While hot, use fingers to sprinkle and smooth the remaining ¼ cup brown sugar on top. Great served warm or chilled. I prefer it warm. Refrigerate unused portions.

Sidebar (Strawberry-Banana Trifle):

Serves 15

0 Fat Grams

With Equal —
Calories: 169
With sugar —
Calories: 173

Sidebar (Tropical Baked Rice Dessert):

♥

Serves 15

0 Fat Grams

Calories: 124

♥ Sweet Cheese Dessert ♥

Not a cheesecake, but resembles one.

Serves 15

.4 Fat Grams

With sugar and NutraSweet Spoonful — Calories: 115
With sugar only — Calories: 131

24 ounces non-fat cottage cheese
1 teaspoon vanilla
1 teaspoon almond extract
5 egg whites
1 whole egg
4 Tablespoons flour (I use 2 whole wheat and 2 all purpose)
2 8-ounce packages fat-free cream cheese (I use Health Valley)
⅔ cup sugar and ⅓ cup NutraSweet Spoonful (OR 1 cup sugar)
1 cup dry pancake mix (I use brand with 2 fat grams per serving. There are many to choose from)

Preheat oven to 350 degrees. Spray a 9 x 13-inch pan with non-fat cooking spray.

Beat cottage cheese 2-3 minutes until smooth and creamy. There may be lumps. Add in remaining ingredients except pancake mix. Beat for 2 minutes, until well blended. Set aside.

Crust:
In a separate bowl, mix the pancake mix with ⅓ cup of the cheese mixture. Press crust mixture gently onto the bottom of the pan. (Do not do sides of pan.)

Pour cheese mixture over crust. Bake for 1 hour or until center is set and top is lightly browned. Cool to room temperature, then refrigerate until chilled thoroughly. If desired, spread 21-ounce can blueberry or cherry pie filling on top before refrigerating.

Refrigerate unused portions.

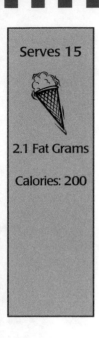

Serves 15

2.1 Fat Grams

Calories: 200

♥ *Pumpkin Crunch Dessert*

This recipe is a mix between a pie and a cake.

1	**box Betty Crocker Super Moist Lite White cake mix — dry**
1	**29-ounce can pumpkin**
2	**teaspoons allspice**
2	**teaspoons cinnamon**
½	**cup brown sugar**

Preheat oven to 350 degrees. Spray 9 x 13-inch pan with non-fat cooking spray. Mix all ingredients listed above in blender and pour into prepared pan.

Excellent Crumb Topping:

¾	**cup brown sugar**
½	**cup quick cooking oats**
¾	**cup whole wheat flour**
½	**teaspoon cinnamon**
3	**Tablespoons Ultra Promise Fat-free margarine, melted**

Mix all ingredients listed above with fork until crumbly. Sprinkle onto cake batter. Bake for 55-60 minutes.

Glaze:

¼	**cup powdered sugar**
2	**teaspoons skim milk**
½	**teaspoon vanilla**

Drizzle glaze over crumb topping, while cake is still warm. Glaze will be thick, but once drizzled on cake, it will thin out.

Refrigerate unused portions.

♥ "Far Out" Fruity Fun Dessert ♥

If you're really in a rush, use 2 store-bought graham cracker crusts.

Serves 12

1.67 Fat Grams

With NutraSweet Spoonful™ — Calories: 149
With sugar — Calories: 169

-6   Tablespoons Fat-free Ultra Promise Margarine
10   graham crackers crushed (each cracker has 4 segments)
¼   cup NutraSweet Spoonful (OR ¼ cup sugar)
1   20-ounce can lite cherry pie filling
1   20-ounce can crushed pineapple in its own juices
1   3-ounce box sugar-free strawberry Jello
3   large bananas, sliced into ¼-inch pieces

Spray 9 x 13-inch pan with non-fat cooking spray. Melt fat-free margarine in microwave. Stir into crushed graham crackers and NutraSweet. Mix well.

Crust:
Press crumb mixture into the bottom of prepared pan. Set aside.

In a 2-quart saucepan, bring cherry pie filling, crushed pineapple with its juices, and Jello to a boil. Boil for 1 minute, stirring constantly. Remove from heat. Add bananas. Pour over graham crackers. Cool in refrigerator for 1 hour. (If using store-bought crust, this will make 2 pies.) Top with Cool Whip Free, if desired. Refrigerate unused portions.

Serves 6

.2 Fat Grams

With Equal —
Calories: 102
With sugar —
Calories: 194

♥ *Strawberry Cream Crunch Fantasy* ♥

Crust:

2   Tablespoons dark brown sugar
2   cups crushed pretzels
1   package Butter Buds, dry
3   Tablespoons water

Preheat oven to 350 degrees. Mix together well. Press into 8-inch cheesecake pan. Bake for 10 minutes.

Filling:

12   ounces fat-free cream cheese
      (I use Kraft Free)
12   packets Equal (OR ½ cup sugar)
1   package Dream Whip

Blend well with mixer on high speed. Spread on cooled pretzel crust.

Strawberry Topping:

1   cup sliced strawberries
4   Packets Equal (or 3 Tablespoons plus 1 teaspoon sugar)
1   cup boiling water
1   package sugar-free strawberry Jello
     (4-serving size)

Slice strawberries and sprinkle with the 4 packets of Equal. Set aside.

Stir sugar-free Jello into 1 cup boiling water. Add strawberries sprinkled with Equal. Chill. When soft set, pour over cream cheese mixture.

Keep complete dessert chilled until ready to serve. Refrigerate unused portions.

Since we can't have the best of everything, it's important to make the best of everything we have.

♥♥♥

♥ *Chocolate Raspberry 000-La-La Dessert* ♥

It's difficult to believe a dessert as special, tasty, and elegant as this can be so easy! A definite hit for a special candlelight dinner!

1	**store-bought, fat-free pound cake** (**approximately 12 oz.**)
8	**teaspoons raspberry preserves**
8	**Tablespoons sugar-free, fat-free chocolate pudding** (**If using a box mix, prepare as directed on box. I use D-Zerta. There will be extra pudding left over. For super easy use, try Hershey's fat-free pudding in the dairy section.**)
8	**Tablespoons Cool Whip Free**

Cut pound cake in half as if making into a two-layer cake. With 2-inch cookie cutter (or biscuit cutter), cut out 8 round pieces from the cake (discard the crumbs) and put each into its own wide mouth (approximately 3-inch across opening) wine glass or pretty dessert cup. Spread 1 teaspoon raspberry preserves on each little cake. Pour 1 Tablespoon chocolate pudding on top of preserves. Top with one Tablespoon Cool Whip.

Presto! You're done! Is this easy or what?! This dessert can be made days ahead and refrigerated until ready to serve. Insert toothpick in middle of each and cover with plastic wrap to keep each dessert creamy and fresh.

If you want to have happy memories — make them now.

Yields 1

.4 Fat Grams

With sugar and NutraSweet Spoonful — Calories: 71
With sugar only — Calories: 81

♥ *Two-In-One Chocolate*
Sandwich Cookie ♥

6	**egg whites**
¼	**cup applesauce**
¼	**cup corn syrup**
2	**teaspoons vanilla**
1¼	**cups evaporated skim milk**
2	**cups whole wheat flour**
1½	**cups all purpose flour**
1	**cup sugar**
½	**cup + 2 Tablespoons NutraSweet Spoonful** (OR 1½ cups + 2 Tablespoons sugar)
1	**cup unsweetened cocoa powder**
½	**cup cornstarch**
1	**Tablespoon baking powder**
1	**teaspoon baking soda**
1½	**teaspoons lite salt**

Preheat oven to 350 degrees. Spray cookie sheet with non-fat cooking spray. Beat egg whites. Add applesauce, corn syrup, vanilla, and evaporated skim milk. Mix well. Add dry ingredients. Mix well in large bowl.

For a plain cookie: Place on prepared cookie sheet by teaspoonfuls. Bake for 5 minutes or until done.

For Sandwich Cookie — Place a dab of marshmallow cream between two cookies.

♥

Yields 2

.8 Fat Grams

With sugar and NutraSweet Spoonful — Calories: 149
With sugar only — Calories: 169

---

*More important than how much money we make is what we **do** with the money we make!*

♥ *Peach Crunch* ♥

9   medium-sized fresh peaches
1   Tablespoon sugar mixed with ½
     teaspoon cinnamon
½   cup whole wheat flour
1¼   cups quick-cooking rolled oats
¾   cup brown sugar packed
2   teaspoons ground cinnamon
     dash of lite salt (optional)
½   cup Ultra Fat-free Promise Margarine

Preheat oven to 350 degrees. Slice peaches, keeping skins
on. Lightly toss peaches with sugar and cinnamon mixture.
Pour into 9 x 13-inch baking pan. Combine oats, flour,
brown sugar, cinnamon, and salt. Cut margarine into
mixture with fork. Place lumpy dough over peaches as
evenly as possible. (Some peach slices will show through.)
Bake for 45-50 minutes. Great served warm with Dream Whip or
non-fat vanilla yogurt. Refrigerate unused portions.

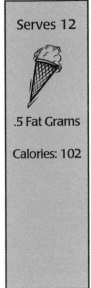

Serves 12

.5 Fat Grams

Calories: 102

♥ *Jelly Roll Cake* ♥

1   box Betty Crocker Super Moist yellow
     cake mix with pudding in the mix — dry
⅓   cup water
6   egg whites (OR ¾ cup Egg Beaters)
20   ounces fruit preserves (Use your favorite
     flavor)

Preheat oven to 350 degrees. Spray two jelly roll pans with
non-fat cooking spray. (A jelly roll pan is a cookie sheet with
1/2-inch sides.) Beat dry cake mix, water, and egg whites in
large bowl on low speed for 30 seconds. Beat on medium
speed for 2 minutes. Pour ½ cup cake batter into each pan and
spread evenly. Bake for 10 minutes. Cool. Spread each cake with
about 7 ounces of preserves.

Roll each cake into a roll, starting from the narrow side. Spread
remaining preserves (about 3 ounces each cake) on top.

♥

Serves 24

2.1 Fat Grams

Calories: 145

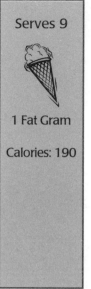

Serves 9

1 Fat Gram

Calories: 190

♥ *Applesauce Spice Squares* ♥

Easy to make and especially good served warm.

³/₄   **cup applesauce**
1½   **cups flour**
1   **cup sugar**
¼   **cup water**
1   **teaspoon baking soda**
³/₄   **teaspoon salt**
¼   **teaspoon cinnamon**
⅛   **teaspoon ground cloves**
⅛   **teaspoon ground allspice**
½   **teaspoon baking powder**
3   **egg whites**
¼   **cup raisins**

Preheat oven to 350 degrees. Spray 9 x 9 x 2-inch pan with non-fat cooking spray. Combine all but raisins in a medium-sized bowl. Mix with electric mixer on high speed for 3 minutes. Pour mixture into prepared pan and add raisins. Bake 30-35 minutes. Cut while warm. Refrigerate unused portions.

♥ *Chocolate Cherry Cookies* ♥

Serves 48

1 Fat Gram
(without
frosting or
chocolate
chips)

Calories: 40

It doesn't get any easier than this super-soft cookie.

1   **box Betty Crocker Super Moist Devil's Food cake mix with pudding in the mix — dry**
1½   **cups lite cherry pie filling**
1   **teaspoon almond extract**
½   **cup chocolate chips, if desired**

Preheat oven to 350 degrees. Spray cookie sheet with non-fat cooking spray. Mix all ingredients well by hand. Drop by teaspoonfuls onto cookie sheet. Bake for 10 minutes. Remove from cookie sheet and cool. (Frost with creamy fat-free chocolate frosting, if desired.) Do not store in airtight container, which may cause cookies to get too soft.

♥ *Harvest Pudding* ♥

Serves 12

.2 Fat Grams

With
NutraSweet
Spoonful —
Calories: 129
With sugar —
Calories: 150

16   egg whites
2⅓   cups skim milk
⅓   cup NutraSweet Spoonful (OR ⅓ cup sugar)
1   12-ounce can of lite evaporated skim milk
½   cup brown sugar, packed
1   teaspoon vanilla
½   teaspoon lite salt
½   teaspoon cinnamon
½   teaspoon ground cloves
8   slices lite (40 calorie) fat-free wheat bread, dried (best if laid out the night before to dry)
½   cup raisins
1   medium apple, chopped thinly, with skin on (approximately ¾ cup)

Preheat oven to 350 degrees. Spray a 9 x 13-inch pan with non-fat cooking spray. Beat together egg whites, milk, NutraSweet, evaporated milk, brown sugar, vanilla, lite salt, cinnamon, and ground cloves. Mix bread, raisins, and apples into egg mixture. Pour into prepared pan. Bake for 40-45 minutes or until a knife inserted near the center comes out clean. Serve warm with spicy cream topping.

Spicy Cream Topping:
1   package Dream Whip
½   cup cold milk
½   teaspoon cinnamon
½   teaspoon ground cloves

Refrigerate unused portions.

Put your love into action.

Serves 24

1.66 Fat Grams

Calories: 104

♥ *Fruit-Filled Snack Squares* ♥

Crust:

1   box Betty Crocker Super Moist yellow cake mix with pudding in the mix — dry
½   cup rolled oats
1   teaspoon cinnamon
⅓   cup applesauce
2   Tablespoons skim milk
2   egg whites

Preheat oven to 350 degrees. Spray 9 x 13-inch pan with non-fat cooking spray. Combine ingredients and beat with mixer on low speed until crumbly. Reserve 1 cup of this mixture. Press remaining mixture into prepared pan. Bake for 15 minutes or until golden brown.

Filling:

1   20-ounce can of your favorite "Lite" pie filling (blueberry, cherry, or apple)

Spread pie filling over crust.

Topping:

½   cup rolled oats
½   teaspoon cinnamon

Combine the 1 cup of mixture reserved earlier with ½ cup rolled oats and ½ teaspoon cinnamon. With fingers, put little dabs of this mixture over top of pie filling. Bake an additional 23-25 minutes or until top is golden brown and pie filling is bubbly. Cool completely before cutting. Refrigerate unused portions.

♥ *Harvest Custard with an Autumn Topping* ♥

I like to serve this warm, but it's also good chilled.

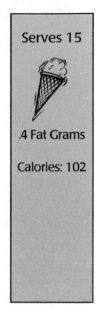

Serves 15

.4 Fat Grams

Calories: 102

8   egg whites
1   16-ounce container fat-free sour cream
6   cups apples, thinly sliced and peeled
¾   teaspoon cinnamon
     Dash of ground cloves
½   cup dark brown sugar
1   teaspoon almond extract

Preheat oven to 325 degrees. Spray a 9 x 13-inch glass casserole dish with non-fat cooking spray. Beat egg whites with fat-free sour cream. Add seasonings and brown sugar. Mix well with blender. Stir in apples until apples are well-coated. Spread apple mixture evenly into pan. Set aside.

Topping:

½   cup Ultra Fat-free Promise Margarine
1   cup quick cooking rolled oats
1   cup dark brown sugar
¼   cup all purpose flour
1   teaspoon cinnamon
     Dash of ground cloves

Cut in margarine with oats, brown sugar, flour, cinnamon, and ground cloves until mixture is well blended. With two forks take little bits of topping and evenly dot top of apple mixture. (Use one fork to push topping mixture off the other fork.)

Set casserole dish in pan containing 1-inch of water. (I use my broiling pan. My casserole dish sits perfectly in it. Try yours.) Bake for 50 minutes or until knife inserted in middle comes out clean. Cool 5 minutes before cutting. Refrigerate unused portions.

♥ *Mincemeat Squares* ♥

A nice change from mincemeat pie for the holidays and a tasty treat any time of the year!

9   **ounces condensed mincemeat** (I use Borden)

1½   **cups water**

2   **cups Jiffy Mix**

¼   **cup NutraSweet Spoonful and ¼ cup sugar**
      (OR ½ cup sugar)

2   **egg whites**

4   **ounces fat-free cream cheese**

Preheat oven to 400 degrees. Spray a 9 x 13-inch pan with a non-fat cooking spray. Set aside.

Crumble mincemeat into 1½ cups water. Bring to a brisk boil and boil for one minute. Set aside. (If you prefer, you can purchase the already prepared filling in a jar. Use two cups.)

In medium-sized bowl, combine Jiffy Mix, NutraSweet, egg whites, and cream cheese. Mix well with blender. Dough will be stiff. Press into bottom of pan, covering it completely.

Spread prepared mincemeat evenly over dough. With fork punch lots of holes through this dessert before baking (to allow some of the juices to seep through the crust). Bake for 27-30 minutes. Cool. Prepare 1 envelope of Dream Whip as directed on box. Spread evenly over cooled mincemeat dessert. Cut into 24 squares. Refrigerate unused portions.

♥ *Pumpkin Bars* ♥

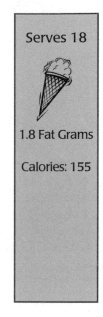

Serves 18

1.8 Fat Grams

Calories: 155

Pumpkin Mixture:

2	teaspoons cinnamon
1	teaspoon pumpkin pie spice
½	cup brown sugar
1	cup pumpkin (from a can)
1	box super moist white cake mix with pudding in the mix (I use Betty Crocker) — dry

Preheat oven to 350 degrees. Spray 9 x 13-inch pan with non-fat cooking spray. Set aside. Mix well all ingredients with blender. Dough will be stiff. Spread with knife into bottom of prepared pan.

Topping:

¼	up Ultra Fat-free Promise Margarine
½	cup quick-cooking rolled oats.
¼	cup brown sugar
1	teaspoon pumpkin pie spice
¼	cup all purpose flour

With a fork, stir margarine into all ingredients until well-blended. Using 2 forks (one fork to push topping off the other fork), spread topping over pumpkin mixture. There will be some spaces where you can see the pumpkin mixture. Bake for 30 minutes or until knife inserted in center comes out clean.

Glaze (optional):

¼	cup powdered sugar
¼	teaspoon pumpkin pie spice
2¼-3	teaspoons milk

When bars have cooled, drizzle glaze over the top. Refrigerate unused portions.

♥ *Fruit Pizzas (Two)* ♥

Serves 24

.3 Fat Grams

With NutraSweet Spoonful —
Calories: 87
With sugar —
Calories: 113

Crust:

2¾   **cups buttermilk pancake mix**
½   **cup sugar**
8   **ounces fat-free cream cheese, softened**
⅓   **cup NutraSweet Spoonful** (OR 1/3 cup sugar)
½   **cup water**

Preheat oven to 350 degrees. Spray 2 13 x 9-inch cookie sheets with non-fat cooking spray. Mix all ingredients until well blended. Press dough with palms to cover bottom of cookie sheets. Bake for 7-10 minutes, until golden brown.

Frosting:

½   **cup NutraSweet Spoonful** (OR ½ cup sugar)
1   **teaspoon almond extract**
2   **8 ounces fat-free cream cheese, softened**
2   **Tablespoons maraschino cherry juice**
      (drain juice from jar of maraschino cherries)

When crust is cool, spread frosting on top and decorate with your choice of fresh fruit. (I like to use kiwi, strawberries, grapes, and oranges.) Refrigerate unused portions.

♥ *No-Fat Pumpkin Cookies* ♥

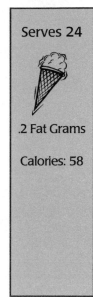

Serves 24

.2 Fat Grams

Calories: 58

1	cup applesauce
1	package Butter Buds, dry (Do not dilute.)
½	cup brown sugar
2	Tablespoons Sugar Twin Brown Sugar Replacement
1	cup canned pumpkin
1	cup all purpose flour
1	cup whole wheat flour
1	teaspoon baking soda
1	teaspoon cinnamon
¼	teaspoon ginger
¼	teaspoon ground cloves
½	teaspoon lite salt

Preheat oven to 375 degrees. Spray cookie sheets with non-fat cooking spray. Mix first five ingredients. Add remaining ingredients and mix well. Drop by teaspoonfuls onto prepared cookie sheets. Bake for 10-12 minutes.

Topping:
3 Tablespoons NutraSweet +
1 Tablespoon cinnamon

Do what you want to do but are afraid to do, in order to obtain what you know you are able to be.

♥♥♥

When cookies have been removed from the oven, spray tops lightly with non-fat cooking spray and gently press top of each cookie into topping. Refrigerate unused portions.

♥ Chocolate Chip Cookies (The Healthy Ones!) ♥

Serves 36

1.7 Fat Grams

With sugar and NutraSweet Spoonful — Calories: 75
With sugar only — Calories: 80

1	package Butter Buds, dry
¼	cup lite corn syrup
½	cup sugar and ¼ cup NutraSweet Spoonful (OR ¾ cup sugar)
5	egg whites
1	teaspoon vanilla
2	cups all purpose flour
1	cup whole wheat flour
1	cup bran (I use oat bran)
1	teaspoon baking soda
1	teaspoon lite salt
1	package (11.5 ounces size) chocolate chips (I use milk chocolate)

Preheat oven to 425 degrees. Spray cookie sheets with non-fat cooking spray. Combine first six ingredients and mix well with mixer on medium speed for 1 minute. Add remaining ingredients except chocolate chips. Mix well. Add chocolate chips. Drop by rounded teaspoonfuls onto cookie sheets. Bake for 8 minutes.

♥ Chewy-Gooey No Bake Freezer Cookies ♥

♥

Serves 36

.3 Fat Grams

Calories: 60

This cookie, like a frozen dessert, will melt. It CANNOT be left out to thaw. Once removed from the freezer, it must be eaten IMMEDIATELY.

2	cups sugar
½	cup skim milk
¼	cup Fat-free Ultra Promise Margarine
3	Tablespoons cocoa
1	teaspoon vanilla
½	cup fat-free cream cheese
3	cups quick cooking oats

Combine first four ingredients in 2-quart saucepan, stirring constantly. Bring to a full boil for 1 minute. Remove from heat, add vanilla, cream cheese and stir until well-blended. Add oats. Drop onto wax paper by the teaspoon. Keep in freezer until ready to eat.

♥ *Rhubarb Pudding* ♥

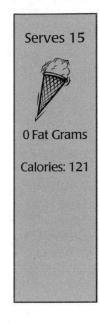
A tasty twist on Bread Pudding! I got this recipe idea from one my Grandma Schaefer had, dated 1906.

5   slices fat-free bread cubed
    (I use Aunt Millie's)
2½ cups fresh rhubarb, diced thinly
5   egg whites
2   cups skim milk
1½ cups brown sugar, packed
1   envelope Butter Buds, dry (Do not add water!)

Preheat oven to 350 degrees. Spray a 9 x 13-inch pan with non-fat cooking spray. Arrange cubed bread and diced rhubarb in prepared pan. Set aside.

In a bowl, beat egg whites until foamy (about 1 minute). Add milk and brown sugar. Beat with mixer on medium speed for 1 minute more. Pour this mixture over bread and rhubarb in pan. With fork make sure mixture saturates all of the bread and rhubarb. Sprinkle top with one envelope of Butter Buds. Bake for 1 hour. Serve warm or cold. When served warm, I like to dab a little Cool Whip Free on the top. Refrigerate unused portions.

♥ Harvest Cookies ♥

Serves 54-60

.75 Fat Grams

With NutraSweet Spoonful —
Calories: 34
With sugar —
Calories: 40

4	**egg whites**
½	**cup NutraSweet Spoonful** (OR ½ cup sugar)
¾	**cup brown sugar**
¼	**cup applesauce**
½	**teaspoon vanilla**
1	**teaspoon baking soda**
½	**teaspoon lite salt**
1	**teaspoon cinnamon**
½	**teaspoon ground cloves or nutmeg**
2	**cups whole wheat flour**
2	**medium apples, peeled and chopped** (approximately 1 cup)
½	**cup chopped nuts** (optional)

Preheat oven to 375 degrees. Spray cookie sheet with non-fat spray. Beat egg whites until foamy. Mix egg whites with NutraSweet, brown sugar, applesauce, and vanilla. Stir in baking soda, salt, cinnamon, ground cloves (or nutmeg) until well mixed. Stir in whole wheat flour, one cup at a time. Mix well. Stir in chopped apples (and nuts if desired). Place teaspoonfuls onto cookie sheet. Bake for 5-6 minutes (until bottoms are golden brown).

Wouldn't it be wonderful if folks were as quick to compliment as they are to criticize?

♥ *Chocolate Cookies* ♥

Yields 96

1.2 Fat Grams

(1) With Sugar and NutraSweet Spoonful — Calories: 56 each
With sugar only — Calories: 60

♥

(2) With sugar and NutraSweet Spoonful — Calories: 42
With sugar only — Calories: 46

(3) With sugar and NutraSweet Spoonful — Calories: 65
With sugar only — Calories: 69

16	egg whites
1	Tablespoon + 1 teaspoon baking powder
1	teaspoon lite salt
⅓	cup applesauce
⅓	cup lite corn syrup
1	Tablespoon + 1 teaspoon vanilla
2½	cups flour
1½	cups sugar and ½ cup NutraSweet Spoonful (OR 2 cups sugar)
4	cups quick cooking oats
1⅓	cups cocoa

(1) Preheat oven to 375 degrees. Spray cookie sheet with non-fat cooking spray. Beat egg whites with baking powder, salt, applesauce, corn syrup, and vanilla until bubbly and lightly foamy. Add remaining dry ingredients. Mix well.

Drop by teaspoonfuls onto prepared cookie sheet. Bake for 9 minutes. Remove cookies from cookie sheet immediately. When cool, store in airtight container.

(2) **Chocolate Chunk Cookies:** Add 1 10-ounce bag semi-sweet chocolate chunks.

(3) **Chocolate Raisin Cookies:** Add 2 cups raisins and 1 10-ounce bag chocolate chunks.

♥ *Spicy Raisin Cookies* ♥

Serves 72

.4 Fat Grams

With
NutraSweet
Spoonful —
Calories: 47
With sugar —
Calories 52

1	cup apple butter (use your favorite brand)
1	cup dark brown sugar
½	cup NutraSweet Spoonful (OR ½ cup sugar)
6	egg whites
1	teaspoon vanilla
1	teaspoon baking soda
1	teaspoon lite salt
1	teaspoon cinnamon
½	teaspoon ground cloves
2	cups whole wheat flour
1	cup self-rising flour
2	cups raisins
⅓	cup chopped pecans

Preheat oven to 375 degrees. Spray a cookie sheet with non-fat cooking spray. Beat first nine ingredients together with mixer at medium speed until well blended. Add both kinds of flour, one cup at a time. By hand, stir in raisins and pecans. Drop by teaspoonful onto prepared cookie sheet. Bake for 7 minutes.

Glaze:

½	cup dark brown sugar
½	cup Healthy Choice fat-free cream cheese
1	teaspoon vanilla

Blend well. Quickly put a thin layer of glaze on cookies while they are still warm.

If you don't at least try to do the thing you've always wanted to do, you'll always wish you had.

♥♥♥

♥ *Itty-Bitty Tea Cookies* ♥

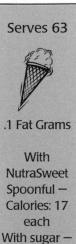

Crust:

- 1⅓ cups buttermilk pancake mix
- ¼ cup sugar and 2 Tablespoons NutraSweet Spoonful (OR ⅓ cup sugar)
- ¼ cup juice from maraschino cherries
- 4 ounces fat-free cream cheese

Preheat oven to 350 degrees. Spray cooking sheet (9½ x 13 ¼-inch) with a non-fat cooking spray. With palm, press dough to cover bottom of pan, to edges of pan. Bake for 7-10 minutes.

Frosting:

- ½ teaspoon almond extract
- ¼ cup NutraSweet Spoonful (OR ¼ cup sugar)
- 8 ounces fat-free cream cheese, softened
- 1 Tablespoon maraschino cherry juice, drained from a jar of maraschino cherries

Beat until smooth and creamy. When cookie has cooled, spread with frosting. After frosted, cut into 63 small pieces. Cut 32 maraschino cherries in half. Place cherry half in each square.

Icing:

- 2 Tablespoons fat-free hot fudge (I use Smucker's)
- 1 teaspoon maraschino cherry juice

Mix and warm hot fudge and cherry juice. With spoon, drizzle over cookies. Refrigerate unused portions.

We have one rule for our home: "Love only." If it's not loving, then don't do it.

Serves 10

1.5 Fat Grams

Calories: 298

♥ *Chocolate-Banana Chocolate Pie* ♥

⅓   **cup cocoa**
⅓   **cup powdered sugar**
1   **8-ounce container Cool Whip Free**

Crust:
8   **ounces chocolate cream sandwich cookies**
     (I use SnackWell's)
3   **Tablespoons liquid Butter Buds**
½   **teaspoon NutraSweet Spoonful**

Spray 9-inch pie pan with non-fat cooking spray. Remove and discard cream filling from chocolate sandwich cookies. In food processor, grind cookies into fine crumbs. Put crumbs in bowl along with 3 Tablespoons liquid Butter Buds and ½ teaspoon NutraSweet Spoonful. Mix well with fork. Press cookie mixture into bottom and along sides of prepared pie pan.

Filling:
3   **bananas (sliced into ¼ inch thickness)**
2   **quarts non-fat chocolate frozen yogurt**
     (set out to thaw while making pie crust)
1   **11.5 ounces fat-free Smucker's hot fudge**
     topping
2   **Tablespoons chocolate chips (optional)**

Arrange banana slices on bottom of pie crust. Spoon as much as possible of the slightly thawed non-fat chocolate frozen yogurt over banana slices. Spoon about ⅔ of Smucker's fat-free hot fudge topping over frozen yogurt. Put into freezer until ready to eat.

Mix together well cocoa, powdered sugar, and Cool Whip Free. Keep refrigerated until ready to eat. When ready to eat, cut pie into 10 pieces and put each piece on its own dessert plate. Top each piece with a dab of the chocolate Cool Whip mixture. Melt remaining hot fudge in microwave and drizzle over each piece of pie. Sprinkle a few chocolate chips on each — if desired.

Although this is a low-fat recipe, it's loaded with calories, so beware! When eating this special treat, remember that moderation is the name of the game.

♥ *Cherry Cobbler* ♥

Serves 12

.6 Fat Grams

With sugar and NutraSweet Spoonful — Calories: 114
With sugar only — Calories: 146

2   cups pie cherries, cleaned and pitted
½   cup sugar and ¼ cup NutraSweet Spoonful (OR ¾ cup sugar)
1   teaspoon cinnamon

Preheat oven to 350 degrees. Mix pie cherries with NutraSweet Spoonful and cinnamon. Pour into 9 x 13-inch baking pan.

2   cups Hungry Jack Pillsbury buttermilk pancake/waffle mix, dry
¼   cup NutraSweet Spoonful
⅔   cup water

Mix well. Dough will be lumpy. With a fork put dough on top of cherry mixture.

Bake approximately 30-35 minutes or until cherries are bubbly and dough is golden brown.

♥ *Chocolate Cherry Brownies* ♥

Serves 32

2.3 Fat Grams

Calories: 161

2   boxes of Lovin' Lites Brownie Mix — dry
1   can lite cherry pie filling
2   egg whites
½   cup chocolate chips

Preheat oven to 350 degrees. Spray 2 — 9 x 13-inch pans with non-fat cooking spray. Mix all ingredients together by hand, about 75 strokes or until well blended. Spread batter into prepared pans. Bake for 25-27 minutes or until cherries are bubbly and dough golden brown.

Immediately after taken out of oven, sprinkle each pan with ¼ cup chocolate chips. Cut each pan into 16 pieces. Refrigerate unused portions.

Serves 12

.6 Fat Grams

With
NutraSweet
Spoonful —
Calories: 97
With sugar
only —
Calories: 112

♥ *Blueberry Cobbler* ♥

⅓ **cup sugar**
½ **teaspoon orange peel**
2 **cups blueberries**
2 **cups Hungry Jack Pillsbury buttermilk pancake/waffle mix, dry**
¼ **cup NutraSweet Spoonful** (OR ¼ cup sugar)
⅔ **cup water**
1 **teaspoon almond extract**

Preheat oven to 350 degrees. Gently stir sugar and orange peel. Add blueberries and stir until well coated. Pour into a 9 x 13-inch baking pan.

Mix pancake mix, NutraSweet, water, and almond extract. Dough will be lumpy. With a fork put dough on top of blueberry mixture. Bake approximately 30-35 minutes or until blueberries are bubbly and dough golden brown. Refrigerate unused portions.

Serves 16

.55 Fat Grams

Calories: 18

♥ *Creamy Spiced Whipped Topping* ♥

1 **package Dream Whip** (A box comes with 4 packages.)
½ **cup cold skim milk**
½ **teaspoon cinnamon**
½ **teaspoon ground cloves**

Combine ingredients and beat with mixer on high for 4 minutes. Keep refrigerated until ready to eat. If you are planning to frost a cake, keep refrigerated until time to frost.

♥ *Blackberry Cobbler* ♥

Super easy — Super yummy

2	**quarts blackberries**
½	**cup sugar and** ¼ **cup NutraSweet Spoonful** (or ¾ cup sugar)
1	**teaspoon cinnamon**
2	**cups pancake mix (I use Staff)**
⅓	**cup sugar and 2 Tablespoons NutraSweet Spoonful** (or ½ cup sugar)

Preheat oven to 350 degrees. Gently mix 2 quarts blackberries with ½ cup sugar and ¼ cup NutraSweet Spoonful. Pour into 9 x 13-inch pan. Sprinkle 1 teaspoon cinnamon on top of sugared berries. Combine 2 cups of Staff pancake mix, ⅓ cup sugar, 2 Tablespoons NutraSweet Spoonful and stir with enough water to make stiff dough. With fork spread on top of berries. Bake 30-35 minutes or until berries are bubbly and dough golden brown.

Serves 12

.4 Fat Grams

With sugar and NutraSweet Spoonful — Calories: 116
With sugar only — Calories: 138

♥ *Cherry Trifle* ♥

1	**cup powdered sugar**
1	**8-ounce package non-fat cream cheese**
1	**8-ounce container non-dairy whipped topping**
¼	**cup chopped pecans or walnuts**
5	**cups cubed angel food cake**
1	**can lite cherry pie filling**

Beat together the powdered sugar and non-fat cream cheese. Add whipped topping and chopped nuts. Stir in angel food cake cubes.

Layer in glass bowl:

½	cake mixture
½	can cherry pie filling

Repeat until all ingredients have been used. Chill for at least 3 hours before serving. Refrigerate unused portions.

♥

Serves 15

1.6 Fat Grams

Calories: 168

♥ *Fruit-Topped Cheesecake* ♥

1	box Betty Crocker Super Moist yellow cake mix with pudding in the mix
8	egg whites
2	Tablespoons applesauce
½	cup + 1 Tablespoon sugar and 2 Tablespoons NutraSweet Spoonful (OR ½ cup minus 1 Tablespoon sugar)
2	8-ounce packages fat-free cream cheese, softened
1½	cups skim milk
3	Tablespoons vanilla
2	Tablespoons lemon juice
1	21-ounce can lite pie filling (cherry or blueberry)

Preheat oven to 300 degrees. Spray 9 x 13-inch pan with non-fat cooking spray. Set aside 1 cup of dry cake mix. In large bowl, mix remaining cake mix, 2 egg whites, and applesauce. Press this mixture evenly into bottom of pan.

Mix NutraSweet Spoonful, sugar, and softened cream cheese. Add 6 egg whites and reserved dry cake mix. Beat with mixer on medium speed for 1 minute. Add milk, vanilla, and lemon juice. Mix until smooth. Pour on top of pressed mixture in pan. Bake for 65-75 minutes or until center is firm. Once cooked, top with pie filling. Chill before serving. Keep refrigerated.

Don't eat your blues away! Choose a hobby, take music lessons, or attend a class in a subject you've always found interesting.

♥♥♥

♥ Lazette's Luscious Strawberry Cheesecake ♥

Serves 20

1.0 Fat Grams

With
NutraSweet —
Calories: 132
With sugar —
Calories: 152

2   quarts strawberries
¼   cup NutraSweet Spoonful (OR ½ cup sugar) to sweeten berries
2   8-ounce fat-free cream cheese
1   8-ounce container fat-free sour cream
1   8-ounce container Cool Whip Free
¾   cup confectioner's sugar and ½ cup NutraSweet Spoonful (OR 1 1½ cups confectioner's sugar)
2   teaspoons vanilla
1   teaspoon almond flavoring
1   10-ounce angel food cake

Mix berries with ¼ NutraSweet Spoonful (or ¼ cup sugar) and set aside.

Beat cream cheese until softened. Stir in sour cream, Cool Whip, confectioner's sugar, vanilla, and almond flavoring (also add ½ cup NutraSweet Spoonful if using the NutraSweet Spoonful recipe).

Cut angel food cake into 2-inch pieces. Combine cake pieces with the creamed mixture until well blended. Layer cream mixture and strawberries in deep glass bowl. Garnish top with whole berries. Refrigerate unused portions.

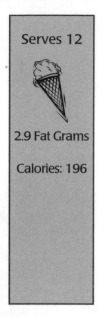

Serves 12

2.9 Fat Grams

Calories: 196

♥ *Three Layer Chocolate Mint Cake* ♥

Seeing the pretty lite green frosting between the layers makes this an extra special beauty!

1	**teaspoon chocolate sprinkles** (optional)
1	**box Betty Crocker Super Moist Devil's Food cake mix with pudding in the mix**
1½	**cups cold skim milk**
3	**packages Dream Whip**
¼	**cup cocoa, sifted**
⅓	**cup powdered sugar, sifted**
	Peppermint extract
	Green food coloring
1	**teaspoon chocolate sprinkles** (optional)

Preheat oven to 350 degrees. Spray 3 8-inch cake pans with non-fat cooking spray. Make cake as directed on package. Pour into prepared cake pans. Bake approximately 12 minutes or until knife inserted in center comes out clean.

Beat 3 packs of Dream Whip with 1½ ups cold skim milk until peaks form. Take ½ of prepared Dream Whip and put into small bowl. Add ½ teaspoon peppermint extract and 3 drops green food coloring. Mix well. Refrigerate cake until it's ready to be frosted.

Add cocoa, powdered sugar, and ½ teaspoon peppermint extract to remainder of prepared Dream Whip.

When cake is completely cool, put first of the 3 baked layers on a cake plate. Frost with ½ of the lite green-colored prepared Dream Whip. Put second layer of cake on top. Frost with the remaining lite green-colored prepared Dream Whip. Put third layer of cake on top. Frost sides of cake with chocolate-colored prepared Dream Whip. Frost top of cake last. Decorate with 1 teaspoon chocolate sprinkles on top of cake (optional).

Cover and keep refrigerated until ready to serve.

♥ *Daddy's Favorite Peach Spice Cake* ♥

This is my husband's favorite cake.

Serves 24

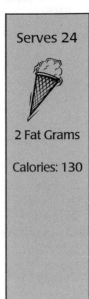

2 Fat Grams

Calories: 130

1½	**cups applesauce**
3	**cups wheat flour**
1	**cup sugar**
1	**cup brown sugar**
½	**cup water**
2	**teaspoons baking soda**
1½	**teaspoons lite salt**
½	**teaspoon cinnamon**
½	**teaspoon ground cloves**
¼	**teaspoon ground allspice**
1	**teaspoon baking powder**
6	**egg whites**
1	**29-ounce can sliced peaches, drained**

Preheat oven to 350 degrees. Spray 9 x 13-inch pan with non-fat spray. Combine all ingredients in a large bowl. Mix with electric mixer for 3 minutes, scraping sides of bowl often.

Pour mixture into prepared pan. Arrange sliced peaches on top of batter pressing each peach slice down so that top of each peach shows and ½ of the peach slice is in batter. Bake 37-47 minutes or until knife inserted in middle comes out clean. Cut while warm.

Spicy whipped topping:

2	**packages Dream Whip**
1	**teaspoon cinnamon**
½	**teaspoon allspice**

Prepare Dream Whip according to directions on the package. Add cinnamon and allspice. Blend into topping. Spoon topping onto cake. Refrigerate unused portions.

The greatest gift in life is to love and to be loved.

♥♥♥

♥ *Very Berry Cake* ♥

1   **cup frozen or fresh berries**
      (I use black raspberries)
1   **Tablespoon NutraSweet Spoonful and** ¼
      cup sugar (OR ⅓ cup sugar)
½   **Tablespoon lemon juice**

Preheat oven to 350 degrees. Spray 8 or 9-inch round cake pan with a non-fat cooking spray. Toss berries with NutraSweet Spoonful. Heat sugar and lemon juice in saucepan until sugar is dissolved.

Arrange berries evenly in prepared pan. Pour dissolved sugar/lemon mixture over berries.

½   **cup whole wheat flour**
½   **cup all purpose flour**
⅓   **cup sugar and 3 Tablespoon NutraSweet**
      Spoonful (OR ½ cup sugar)
2   **teaspoons baking powder**
½   **teaspoon lite salt**
4   **egg whites**
½   **cup water**
⅓   **cup applesauce**
1   **teaspoon vanilla**

Mix all ingredients listed above by hand until smooth. Carefully pour cake batter over berries. Bake 30 minutes or until toothpick inserted in center comes out clean. As soon as you take cake out of oven, run knife around outer edge of cake pan and invert cake onto serving plate.

This cake can be frozen, then warmed in the microwave and served with Dream Whip, vanilla non-fat frozen yogurt or Cool Whip Free. Refrigerate unused portions.

♥ *Pineapple Upside Down Cake* ♥

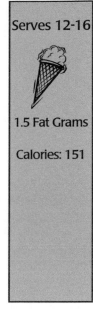

Serves 12-16

1.5 Fat Grams

Calories: 151

1	**20-ounce can crushed pineapple, in its own juice**
3	**egg whites**
1	**box lite white cake mix** (I use Betty Crocker's Super Moist)
¼	**cup fat-free Ultra Promise margarine**
1	**cup dark brown sugar, packed**
12	**maraschino cherries, cut in half**

Preheat oven to 350 degrees. Spray a 9 x 13-inch pan with non-fat spray. Drain as much juice from pineapple as possible. Beat egg whites, pineapple juice, and cake mix with mixer for 30 seconds on low speed, then 2 minutes on medium speed. Set aside.

Melt fat-free margarine and brown sugar over low heat in medium-sized pan until smooth and creamy. Pour melted sugar and margarine mixture into prepared pan so that the whole bottom of pan is covered. With fingers press crushed pineapple and maraschino cherries into sugar/margarine mixture. Pour prepared cake batter over pineapple and cherries.

Bake for 35 minutes or until knife inserted in middle comes out clean and top of cake is golden brown. Immediately run spatula around edge of pan. Cool in pan for 5 minutes. Invert onto a plate. Refrigerate unused portions.

♥ A+ Pumpkin Cake ♥

Serves 15

2.1 Fat Grams

With
NutraSweet
Spoonful —
Calories: 169
With sugar
only —
Calories: 185

This cake is absolutely delicious served warm with a glob of creamy spiced whipped topping on each piece. Once cooled you can frost the cake with the same creamy spiced whipped topping. Keep refrigerated. It's excellent served chilled!

4	egg whites
⅔	cup lite brown sugar
⅓	cup NutraSweet Spoonful (OR ⅓ cup sugar)
1	teaspoon ground cinnamon
½	teaspoon nutmeg
½	teaspoon allspice
1	16-ounce can pumpkin
1	box lite yellow cake mix
	(I use Betty Crocker's Super Moist)

Preheat oven to 350 degrees. Spray a 9 x 13-inch cake pan with non-fat cooking spray. Beat egg whites 15 seconds. Add brown sugar, NutraSweet Spoonful, ground cinnamon, nutmeg, allspice, and pumpkin. Mix until well blended. Add cake mix. Beat with mixer for one minute on high speed. Bake for 37-40 minutes. Refrigerate unused portions.

Exercise your nose; take time to smell the flowers.

♥ *Where the Goo Goes* ♥

If you like pineapple upside down cake and cheesecake, you'll like this clever combination. I got this idea from my Grandma, Jerri Seibert.

Serves 15

1.5 Fat Grams

With powdered sugar and NutraSweet Spoonful — Calories: 150

With powdered sugar only — Calories: 163

Crust:
- 11 **graham crackers** (each graham cracker has 4 segments)
- ⅓ **cup Fat-free Ultra Promise Margarine**
- 2 **Tablespoons sugar**

Preheat oven to 350 degrees. Spray a 9 x 13-inch pan with a non-fat cooking spray. With food processor grind graham crackers until they are fine crumbs. Melt fat-free margarine in microwave (about 15 seconds). Mix sugar. Press into prepared pan. Bake for 10 minutes. Cool.

Cream Filling:
- 1 **envelope Dream Whip**
- ½ **cup cold skim milk**
- 1 **teaspoon almond extract**
- 2 **8-ounce packages fat-free cream cheese, softened to room temperature** (I use Healthy Choice)
- ½ **cup powdered sugar** (OR use ¼ cup NutraSweet Spoonful + 2 Tablespoons powdered sugar)

Beat 1 envelope Dream Whip with ½ cup cold skim milk and almond extract with mixer for 4 minutes on high speed. Add softened cream cheese and powdered sugar. Smooth cream mixture over cooled crust.

Topping:
- 1 **20-ounce can crushed pineapple, with its juices**
- 2 **Tablespoons cornstarch**
- 3 **Tablespoons brown sugar**

With whisk, mix well until cornstarch is completely dissolved. Turn heat to medium. Bring to a boil, stirring occasionally. Boil for 1 minute. Remove from heat. Cool. Spread on top of cheese mixture. Refrigerate for 2 hours before serving. Refrigerate unused portions.

♥ *Radiant Rhubarb Cake* ♥

3   cups fresh rhubarb, sliced into thin ¼-inch
    pieces
¾   cup water
1   cup sugar
1   box strawberry sugar-free Jello, dry
    (4-serving size)
6   egg whites
1⅓ cups water
1   box lite yellow cake mix (I use Betty Crocker
    Super Moist Lite) — dry
2   cups mini marshmallows

Preheat oven to 350 degrees. Spray a 9 x 13-inch pan with a
non-fat cooking spray. Over medium heat in a saucepan bring
the rhubarb, ¾ cup water and sugar to a boil. Boil 3 minutes.
Remove from heat. Add strawberry Jello, dry. (Do not prepare as
directed on box.) Cool.

Beat egg whites until bubbly (about 1 minute). Add 1⅓ cup water
and box of lite cake mix. Beat with mixer for 2 minutes on medium
speed.

Arrange the mini marshmallows on bottom of prepared pan. Pour
cake batter evenly over marshmallows. Spoon the lightly cooled
rhubarb on top of cake batter. Bake for 40 minutes. Serve warm or
cold. (I like it best warm!)

As this bakes, the marshmallows will rise to the top of the cake.
Frosting is not needed. If serving warm, I like to put a dab of Cool
Whip Free on it! Refrigerate unused portions.

♥ *No Bake Eclair Cake* ♥

I like this best when prepared 2-3 days before eating.

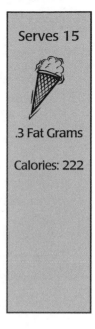

Serves 15

.3 Fat Grams

Calories: 222

- **2** **envelopes Dream Whip, prepared as directed**
- **2** **3.4 ounce boxes of French vanilla pudding** (it has to be French vanilla!) **prepared as directed on box**
- ½ **jar Smucker's Fat-free Hot Fudge** (11.5 ounce size) **Whole graham crackers**

Prepare both Dream Whip and pudding as directed. Refrigerate for 5 minutes. Line a 9 x 13-inch pan with whole graham crackers. Seven and a half whole graham crackers (each including 4 sections) will be needed to cover the bottom of the pan.

Mix pudding and Dream Whip together until well blended. Pour ½ of the pudding/Dream Whip mixture on top of graham crackers. Put another layer of 7½ whole graham crackers on top of pudding/Dream Whip mixture.

Put remaining pudding/Dream Whip mixture on top of graham crackers. Put 7½ whole graham crackers on top of pudding/Dream Whip mixture.

The cake should be layered in the following order:

7½ graham crackers

½ pudding/Dream Whip mixture

7½ graham crackers

remainder pudding/Dream Whip mixture

7½ graham crackers

hot fudge

Frost top layer of graham crackers with hot fudge that has been microwaved for a few seconds, so that it will spread easier. Refrigerate. Serve chilled. Refrigerate unused portions.

About the Author

Dawn Hall is the oldest of seven children. As a youngster, she was proud of how much she could eat, and the kids she grew up with had contests to see who could eat the most. It wasn't long before she was a food addict, and she began a lifelong struggle with weight control and related health issues.

Dawn and her husband, Tracy, were high school sweethearts. He was the captain of the basketball team, and she — despite her problem with overeating — was the homecoming queen. They married, had two children, and had just built their own home when Tracy was diagnosed with a brain tumor. He was given a 10 percent chance of living five years, but has since returned to work as a tool and die maker part time, cycled up to 32 miles in one day, and has even gone white-water rafting!

Besides authoring *Down Home Cookin' Without the Down Home Fat*, Dawn is an accomplished aerobics instructor and facilitator for W.O.W. (Watching Our Weight). She has also home schooled her children. Her church-related work is commendable, particularly her contributions to an organization called Solid Rock, an inner city children's and youth ministry in Toledo. A percentage of her profits from the sale of this cookbook goes to this outreach.

Dawn is a popular inspirational speaker and a veteran talk-show guest. She has appeared on "The 700 Club," "Woman to Woman," "Good Morning Saturday A.M.," various cooking programs, and numerous radio programs. Her public appearances reflect her private life: full of energy, insight, and creative ideas for living a great life — no matter what your circumstances!

To contact the author, or for further information,
call, write, or fax:

Dawn Hall
5425 S. Fulton-Lucas Road
Swanton, Ohio 43558
419-826-2665 (phone)
419-826-2700 (fax)

YOU CAN USE THIS BOOK
AS A FUND-RAISER!

Tracy and Dawn sold 18,000 copies within ten weeks in order to pay for medical treatment, travel expenses for treatment, vitamins, etc. that insurance does not pay for.

Now the book is available for *other patients* who need to raise extra money for the rising expenses that insurance will not cover. Write, fax or phone Cozy Homestead Publishing at:

5425 South Fulton-Lucas Road
Swanton, OH 43558
Phone: (419) 826-2665
Fax: (419) 826-2700

Let them know your request to use the cookbook as a fund-raiser. Upon approval, ideas to successfully run your fund-raiser will be sent.

If the fund-raising group would like books on loan, you can purchase books with VISA, MasterCard and Discover, which would give you time to sell the books in order to pay for them before you receive the charge. Or if you'd like, you can pay with a cashier's check or money order for the actual book cost. Discounts are available for bulk purchases.

BOOK FOR A BUCK!

A 127-page book titled
The Message of Hope
by NavPress

In this book, you will find information on how to obtain God's free gifts of peace, love, and joy in your life along with eternal salvation.

Of all the gifts I've received in my life, His gifts are the most valuable to me! I want to share them with you.

Please mail $1.00 per book (to help cover cost) along with this form.

Name _____

Address _____

City/State _____

Zip Code _____

Mail to: COZY HOMESTEAD PUBLISHERS, INC.
Attn.: FB Dept.
5425 South Fulton-Lucas Road
Swanton, OH 43558

COOKBOOK ORDER FORM

"Down Home Cookin' Without the Down Home Fat!"

These COOKBOOKS make GREAT Gifts! Stock up and keep some on hand (for those last minute gifts).

Look at the chart below for cost of book

Qty.	Item	Cost Per Book	Total
	Down HOME Cookin Without the Down Home Fat by Aunt Dawn		
	OH residents add 6.25%Sales Tax per book		
	Add $2 per book-shipping & handling ($3 if only 1 book)		
	Total		

Fill out and send this order form with payment to:
Cozy Homestead Publishing
5425 S. Fulton-Lucas Rd, Swanton, OH 43558
VISA, Mastercard, and Discover are Welcome
Call Toll Free 1-888-436-9646

Name _____

Address _____

City_____State_____Zip_____

Credit Card/Acct# _____Exp. Date_____

Signature _____

Discounts

# of books	Cost per book	Total cost for all books	2 or more books equal $2 per bk. shipping	Total cost
1	$17.95	$17.95	$3.00°	$20.95
2	$12.95	$25.90	$4.00	$29.90
3 or more	$10.95	$32.85	$6.00	$38.85

°if only 1 book

3 or more books are $10.95 each plus $2.00 per book shipping & handling